DRACULA OF PENNSYLVANIA

A full-length dramedy by
Don Goodrum

www.youthplays.com
info@youthplays.com
424-703-5315

Dracula of Pennsylvania © 2014 Don Goodrum
All rights reserved. ISBN 978-1-62088-571-0.

Caution: This play is fully protected under the copyright laws of the United States of America, Canada, the British Commonwealth and all other countries of the copyright union and is subject to royalty for all performances including but not limited to professional, amateur, charity and classroom whether admission is charged or presented free of charge.

Reservation of Rights: This play is the property of the author and all rights for its use are strictly reserved and must be licensed by the author's representative, YouthPLAYS. This prohibition of unauthorized professional and amateur stage presentations extends also to motion pictures, recitation, lecturing, public reading, radio broadcasting, television, video and the rights of adaptation or translation into non-English languages.

Performance Licensing and Royalty Payments: Amateur and stock performance rights are administered exclusively by YouthPLAYS. No amateur, stock or educational theatre groups or individuals may perform this play without securing authorization and royalty arrangements in advance from YouthPLAYS. Required royalty fees for performing this play are available online at www.YouthPLAYS.com. Royalty fees are subject to change without notice. Required royalties must be paid each time this play is performed and may not be transferred to any other performance entity. All licensing requests and inquiries should be addressed to YouthPLAYS.

Author Credit: All groups or individuals receiving permission to produce this play must give the author(s) credit in any and all advertisements and publicity relating to the production of this play. The author's billing must appear directly below the title on a separate line with no other accompanying written matter. The name of the author(s) must be at least 50% as large as the title of the play. No person or entity may receive larger or more prominent credit than that which is given to the author(s) and the name of the author(s) may not be abbreviated or otherwise altered from the form in which it appears in this Play.

Publisher Attribution: All programs, advertisements, flyers or other printed material must include the following notice:
Produced by special arrangement with YouthPLAYS (www.youthplays.com).

Prohibition of Unauthorized Copying: Any unauthorized copying of this book or excerpts from this book, whether by photocopying, scanning, video recording or any other means, is strictly prohibited by law. This book may only be copied by licensed productions with the purchase of a photocopy license, or with explicit permission from YouthPLAYS.

Trade Marks, Public Figures & Musical Works: This play may contain references to brand names or public figures. All references are intended only as parody or other legal means of expression. This play may also contain suggestions for the performance of a musical work (either in part or in whole). YouthPLAYS has not obtained performing rights of these works unless explicitly noted. The direction of such works is only a playwright's suggestion, and the play producer should obtain such permissions on their own. The website for the U.S. copyright office is *http://www.copyright.gov*.

COPYRIGHT RULES TO REMEMBER

1. To produce this play, you must receive prior written permission from YouthPLAYS and pay the required royalty.

2. You must pay a royalty each time the play is performed in the presence of audience members outside of the cast and crew. Royalties are due whether or not admission is charged, whether or not the play is presented for profit, for charity or for educational purposes, or whether or not anyone associated with the production is being paid.

3. No changes, including cuts or additions, are permitted to the script without written prior permission from YouthPLAYS.

4. Do not copy this book or any part of it without written permission from YouthPLAYS.

5. Credit to the author and YouthPLAYS is required on all programs and other promotional items associated with this play's performance.

When you pay royalties, you are recognizing the hard work that went into creating the play and making a statement that a play is something of value. We think this is important, and we hope that everyone will do the right thing, thus allowing playwrights to generate income and continue to create wonderful new works for the stage.

Plays are owned by the playwrights who wrote them. Violating a playwright's copyright is a very serious matter and violates both United States and international copyright law. Infringement is punishable by actual damages and attorneys' fees, statutory damages of up to $150,000 per incident, and even possible criminal sanctions. **Infringement is theft. Don't do it.**

Have a question about copyright? Please contact us by email at info@youthplays.com or by phone at 424-703-5315. When in doubt, please ask.

CAST OF CHARACTERS

DRAKE PRESCOTT, male, 14. Drake is a fragile boy with a vivid imagination and an over-developed sense of guilt and responsibility. He is an outsider who doesn't have many friends and finds it difficult to relate to other people.

MICHAEL PRESCOTT, male, 40-45. Drake's father. He is a kind and well-meaning father, so overcome by his own grief and his own problems that he has no idea how to help his son.

DR. VIVIAN MARQUETTE, female, 45-65. Of European descent, Vivian means well, but has a hard time understanding these emotional Americans. She is always dressed for business unless otherwise noted and is not overly emotional with Drake or anyone else.

WYSTERIA BELLADONNA NIGHTSHADE/AIMEE STRINGER, female, 16. Spacy and new-aged, Wysteria wears lots of flowing, old-fashioned looking clothing, primarily in black and red. An outsider herself with an equally vivid imagination, Wysteria probably doesn't believe Drake is really a vampire, but she fully supports his right to say he is anyway.

DR. MEGATRON VON FUNKENSTEIN/BILLY, male, 16. Having suffered a deeply emotional loss as a young boy, Dr. Funk is obsessed with the occult and tales from beyond the grave. Defensive and prickly, he wears his heart on his sleeve and, in his own way, is as fragile as Drake.

BIT GIRL/CHERYL, female, 15-16. The heart and, more importantly, the common sense of the Agents of GEEK, Bit Girl is very sensible and grounded and does what she can to keep Dr. Funk in check. She is the resident hacker of the group.

HOWLING TOMMY, male, 16. The strong and silent type, he is Dr. Funk's best friend and bodyguard. He is totally devoted to Dr. Funk and would do anything for him.

WHINER/DAWN, female, 15. An impressionable young girl with poor social skills, Whiner latched onto Dr. Funk and his crew in elementary school and hasn't yet found the courage to leave them behind, even though she no longer has much in common with them. Earnest but not very bright, she looks up to Bit Girl and has lost faith in Dr. Funk's leadership.

AMANDA CLAYPOOL, female, 17. A born politician and/or used car salesman, Amanda is one of those people who truly want to help you, whether you like it or not. Aggressive to the point of rudeness and more than a little narcissistic, she generally gets what's coming to her, even though she seldom knows or understands why.

PENELOPE WINKLE, female, 15. Amanda's minion. Penelope is completely devoted to Amanda and looks up to her until the end of the play when she realizes just how misguided and self-serving Amanda's philanthropy can be.

TWO POLICE OFFICERS, any age, any gender. Two nondescript police officers in uniform. Cast as necessary.

THE ANGRY MOB, various. Appearing in two scenes, the mob can contain anywhere from five to twenty people. They are the folks in line for the movie at the end of Act I and the folks who mob around Drake's house at the end of Act II. Angry and clueless, they can be played by stage hands and anyone else you happen to have hanging around.

NOTES

Toward the middle of Act II, as Drake's therapist tries to uncover the reason for his guilt over his mother's death, Drake uses the word "bitch." It is a pivotal moment in the main character arc of the play and if you can leave the word in, by all means, please do. If, however, you work with one of those schools or theatres who does not allow profanity of any kind in their shows, you have my permission to change the line from "I called her a bitch" to "I told her I hated her and that I didn't love her anymore!" This is the only line you can sub with. I realize it's not as strong as the original, but it does work and I will allow it if there is no other choice.

THE GEEKS: The Agents of GEEK are meant to be comic foils for Drake, dressed in silly costumes with silly toys, but you need to treat them like real people with real lives all the same. Never go so far afield with any of them that it dilutes the impact of their own personal history and introspection (especially Billy). Their costumes should be outlandish and "sci-fi" looking and their weapons and instruments should begin with toys like water guns and nerf guns or any toy that lights up or makes a noise and you can paint or add to them from there. Just don't let the actors use them to distract from the emotional moments of the play. These characters carry their own emotional weight that is intended to heighten the impact of the play if used properly.

ACKNOWLEDGEMENTS

Dracula of Pennsylvania was originally produced by The Theatre Project at South Walton High School in Santa Rosa Beach, Florida, October 30-31 and November 1, 2014. It was directed by Don Goodrum and featured:

Jordyn Felker as Drake Prescott
Savannah Whitten as Wysteria Belladonna Nightshade
Satchel Petterson as Michael Prescott
Alaina Staniewicz as Dr. Vivian Marquette
Isaac Harris as Dr. Funk
Alexis Guessford as Bit Girl
Stephen Fontana as Howling Tommy
Marley Davis as Whiner
Brooke Pierson as Amanda Claypool
Olivia Mullins as Penelope Winkle
Gage McGoff and Levi Stone as the Policemen
Emma Hanley, Isabelle Dye, Savanna Kelley, Hannah Calderazzo, Logan Lawrence, Racquel Lombardo, Jillian Goldberg, Abby Thurston, Shelby Maxwell, Lexie Chadwick, Haley Peters, Megan Shrewsbury, Elizabeth Buckner, Kara Glover and Chloe Bandy as the Angry Mob.

As always, this play is dedicated to my darling daughters, Blayre, Brittany and Sara and my equally darling granddaughters, Claudia and Rori.

Special thanks goes to my former student Aimee Thorgaard, who in many ways inspired the character of Wysteria, my students at South Walton High School for embracing this play with such enthusiasm and bringing it to life, Jeremy Ribando and Nancy Hasty for the professional feedback and the Reading Rangers, Mark Murphy, Dave Chancellor, Ken Preuss and others, for once again being the first line of defense in the war to save the world from bad plays (or, at the very least, my bad plays). There is room in my post-apocalyptic bunker for you all.

ACT I

SCENE 1

(The show begins on the apron, with the curtain closed. A spotlight appears Center and the air is filled with a driving musical beat. [See notes.] The curtain parts [but doesn't open] and four figures enter Center Stage: DR. MEGATRON VON FUNKENSTEIN, HOWLING TOMMY, BIT GIRL and WHINER. They are the Agents of GEEK and will act as both the antagonists and narrators of our story. As the music continues, they take positions on the apron and begin moving to the rhythm of the music as they begin rapping.)

DR. FUNK: *(Rapping to the music:)* WHEN THE NIGHT GETS DARK AND THE WORLD GETS

ALL: SCARY!

DR. FUNK: ARE YOU FEELING PRETTY NERVOUS? ALL THE GIRLS SAY

BIT GIRL AND WHINER: VERY!

TOMMY: WHEN THE BOOGEY MAN'S GOT YOU AND YOU CAN'T EVEN

ALL: SPEAK!

TOMMY: WHO YOU GONNA CALL? THE AGENTS OF —

(Dr. Funk is suddenly unhappy about something and starts trying to shut everyone up as the group chants.)

ALL EXCEPT DR. FUNK: GEEK! GEEK! THE AGENTS OF GEEK! DON'T BE SUCH A BABY AND TRY NOT TO FREAK!

DR. FUNK: Quiet, you guys! Shut up and knock it off! QUIET!

(There is a loud record scratch and everyone but Bit Girl stops.)

BIT GIRL: *(Oblivious to the fact that everyone else has stopped chanting:)* FEE FI FO FO FUM! YOU GET IN MY FACE, I'LL MAKE YOU SWALLOW YO' GUM!

(She starts beat-boxing and dancing.)

DR. FUNK: Bit Girl! Knock it off!

(Bit Girl stops dancing and looks around.)

BIT GIRL: Huh? Oh, were we finished? What happened?

DR. FUNK: I'll tell you what happened! *(To Howling Tommy:)* I have told you and told you that we can't use the phrase "*Who you gonna call?*"! That's a trademarked slogan for another group! Do you want to get sued?

ALL EXCEPT DR. FUNK: No...

DR. FUNK: Do you all want me to take my stuff and go home?

ALL EXCEPT DR. FUNK: No...

WHINER: Jeez, Billy...

DR. FUNK: *(Turning on her:)* And I have also told you a million times, Whiner, my name is *not* Billy! When we are in uniform and in action mode, I am Dr. Megatron Von Funkenstein! Is that clear?

ALL EXCEPT DR. FUNK: Yes...

DR. FUNK: Alrighty then. Let's start over —

ALL EXCEPT DR. FUNK: *(As the music starts again:)* GEEK! GEEK! THE AGENTS OF GEEK!

DR. FUNK: No, no! Stop!

(Record scratch again and music and chanting stop.)

I don't mean start all the way over! I mean —

(He gives up and turns to face the audience with an awkward bow.)

Welcome fellow humans, parents and other mutants and sub-creatures. I am Dr. Megatron Von Funkenstein and we are The Agents of GEEK. That's G-E-E-K, the Ghostly Examination and Elimination Krewe!

TOMMY: I thought "crew" started with a "C."

(The others nod and mumble in agreement.)

DR. FUNK: "K" is the French spelling. You know, like Mardi Gras.

BIT GIRL: Mardi Gras starts with a K?

DR. FUNK: No! Krewe as in Mardi —

(He gives up and turns back to the audience.)

Ladies and gentlemen, as you can see, I do not venture into the dark world of the paranormal alone! Allow me to introduce my associates: Howling Tommy, Master of the Sonic Howl!

(Tommy howls like a wolf.)

Bit Girl, Commander of the Keyboard!

BIT GIRL: *(Wiggling her fingers across her laptop:)* That's Commander with a "K!"

DR. FUNK: And Whiner, who...whines —

WHINER: *(Whining:)* Hey, what do you hafta pick on me for?

DR. FUNK: — a lot. And it is our task, sentient beings, to usher you into this World of the Unknown, this Domain of the Dead! To explain to you what *has* happened, what *does* happen and what *will* happen —

BIT GIRL: Sorta like a Geek Chorus!

DR. FUNK: —in the macabre case of Drake Prescott, insignificant freshman at East Side High, drowned in a sea of tragedy to rise up into the undead majesty of the night!

WHINER: Drowned? Who drowned? I thought we were chasing vampires! *(Pouting:)* Nobody ever tells me nothin'!

DR. FUNK: Hit it, Tommy!

(Tommy howls furiously and the music begins again as The Agents of GEEK clear. All but Whiner go off SL. Whiner goes off SR, then realizes she's going the wrong way and races back SL to exit with the rest.)

SCENE 2

(The stage clears and the curtain opens just wide enough to reveal the front stoop of the Prescott home. It can be very simple; a door and a couple of steps. Entering SR is DR. VIVIAN MARQUETTE. Dr. Marquette walks with purpose up to the door, wearing sensible shoes and a simple business suit and carrying a briefcase. As she gets to the door, it opens and MICHAEL PRESCOTT emerges. Dressed in jeans and a sweater, he has an anxious, worried expression on his face. He hurries out the door and meets Dr. Marquette.)

MICHAEL: *(Shaking her hand:)* Dr. Marquette! So nice to finally meet you in person. I'm Michael Prescott.

VIVIAN: It's nice to meet you.

MICHAEL: I'm sorry to meet you out here on the stoop, but I wanted to talk to you for a moment before Drake knows you're here.

VIVIAN: Is there a problem?

MICHAEL: *(Laughing wryly:)* A problem? My wife is dead and my son thinks he's a vampire.

VIVIAN: Of course. Forgive me. I meant to ask if there is a problem here and now? One that prevents me from entering the house?

MICHAEL: No, I just wanted to catch you for a moment to thank you for making a house call—

VIVIAN: *(Interrupting:)* Just so long as you understand that the arrangement is strictly temporary, Mr. Prescott. As I told you at the hospital, I will rearrange my schedule and meet with Drake here for the first couple of weeks, but then he must commit to his recovery by agreeing to meet me at my office.

MICHAEL: I understand. And please call me Michael. I have a feeling we'll be seeing quite a bit of each other.

VIVIAN: Thank you, Michael. And you may call me Dr. Marquette. May I come inside and meet your son? I'd like to get started.

MICHAEL: Of course, I just wanted to be sure—

VIVIAN: Mr. Prescott. Michael. *(She softens for the first time.)* I understand that you and your son are living a horrible nightmare. But no journey can come to an end without first being begun. May we go inside now? Your hour has started.

MICHAEL: Of course. *(He stops.)* Ah, you're not wearing a cross, are you? Or anything silver? Drake has a real thing these days about crosses.

VIVIAN: *(Opening her collar, exposing her throat:)* No crosses, no silver. I am, however, carrying three wooden stakes and a sprig of wolfsbane in my briefcase. *(She pauses as Michael stares at her in horror.)* I'm kidding, Michael. *(Gesturing to the door:)* May we?

MICHAEL: Sure. Welcome to my home, Dr. Van Helsing.

(Vivian stops and looks at him for a moment, as he smiles awkwardly at his joke.)

(She steps into the house and Michael follows. Once they walk through, the curtains open fully and the front stoop is rolled away.)

SCENE 3

(As the curtains open, we see Drake's bedroom. It is a typical bedroom for a 14-year-old boy with a bed on the UR corner, a desk and chest of drawers along the UC wall and a door to the hallway in the UL corner. A window, covered by heavy drapes is on the SR wall. There are posters on the walls of sports figures and movies, particularly one or two for horror films. There is a computer on the desk and models and other items scattered about the furniture and shelves.)

(Lying on the bed is DRAKE PRESCOTT. Wearing all black with his hands crossed over his chest in a funereal pose, he stares at the ceiling until he hears a dog howl from outside. He rises, unsuccessfully trying to be graceful, and steps to the window, pushing the curtain aside to look out. As he looks, the dog howls again.)

DRAKE: *(As the howling continues:)* Ah, the creatures of the night! What beautiful music —

OFFSTAGE VOICE: Would somebody shut that blasted dog up?

(Crashing sound as something falls outside.)

DRAKE: OK, maybe not so musical after all.

(He sighs heavily as someone knocks on the door.)

MICHAEL: *(Sticking his head through the door:)* Drake? Are you decent? Dr. Marquette is here.

DRAKE: *(Lowering his voice, trying to sound mysterious:)* Enter and be forewarned, human. I am here.

(Michael enters hesitantly, but Vivian pushes past him, entering forcefully and crossing C.)

VIVIAN: *(Holding her hand out for him to shake:)* Hello, Drake. I am Dr. Marquette. I am here to help you.

DRAKE: *(Ignoring her proffered hand:)* Good evening, Doctor. While I appreciate your intentions, I am afraid they are misplaced. I am already a monster, undead and damned. There is no help for me.

VIVIAN: Hmm, we shall see. *(She turns to Michael.)* Mr. Prescott, if you will excuse us?

MICHAEL: Certainly. If there's anything you need—?

VIVIAN: We need you to wait outside. I will let you know when we're finished. Thank you.

MICHAEL: *(Backing out the door:)* Oh, uh, sure. I'll, uh, be out, um...

> *(Vivian closes the door in his face and he finishes his sentence from the other side of the door.)*

...here.

VIVIAN: So, may we sit?

DRAKE: Human comforts are beyond me, mortal, but if you wish to sit, you may.

> *(Vivian grabs a chair from the desk and pulls it DC in front of him.)*

VIVIAN: Drake, my accent and manner are both ingrained and can't be helped. Yours, however, are affected and worn as poorly as an elephant wears a tutu.

> *(Drake looks at her strangely.)*

Sorry. That was something my father used to say. What I mean is, can we just talk like two normal people? Like friends?

> *(Drake's attitude deflates and he sits hunched over on the bed.)*

DRAKE: Yes ma'am.

VIVIAN: *(Sitting and pulling a pen and a notebook from her purse, which she opens:)* Shall we get to it then?

(He nods.) Now then tell me, is there anything you'd like to talk about?

DRAKE: *(Flat and emotionless:)* No.

VIVIAN: Nothing at all? Everything's okay?

DRAKE: *(Sarcastically:)* Just peachy.

VIVIAN: Drake, you have to tell me the truth if you want me to help you.

DRAKE: You can't help me. I'm a monster. Period. That's all there is to it.

VIVIAN: That is what you believe?

DRAKE: That's what is. What I believe has nothing to do with it.

VIVIAN: Hmm. And you drink human blood?

DRAKE: I will, once my transformation is complete.

VIVIAN: Ah, and when will this completion take place?

DRAKE: When I am so overcome by my inhuman hunger that I attack someone and drain them.

VIVIAN: And are you feeling hungry now?

DRAKE: *(Smiling, trying to seem dangerous:)* You'd better hope not.

(Vivian rises and crosses SL, thinking.)

VIVIAN: *(Turning back to him:)* Do you have fangs?

DRAKE: Not until my first feeding.

VIVIAN: *(Crossing back to stand behind chair:)* And can you turn into a bat?

DRAKE: No. Metamorphosis is an advanced ability and doesn't develop until I've been undead for at least one hundred years.

VIVIAN: I had no idea there were so many rules. Can you fly?

DRAKE: No, I can't fly. I'm not Superman.

VIVIAN: What *can* you do, then?

DRAKE: *(Ruefully:)* I can kill.

VIVIAN: *(Making a note:)* Ah yes, the killing. Back to that.

DRAKE: *(Looking at his feet:)* Yes. Back to that.

VIVIAN: *(A beat, as she sits:)* Tell me about your mother.

DRAKE: *(His head snaps up to look at her sharply.)* My mother?

VIVIAN: Yes, your mother. Tell me about the accident.

(Drake stands and crossed DR as he composes himself.)

DRAKE: Why do you want to know about the accident?

VIVIAN: Because I am trying to get to know you; to understand what's happened to you. Please tell me what happened.

DRAKE: *(Flat and emotionless again:)* There's nothing to tell. My mother and I were driving into Philadelphia to buy me some school clothes. There was an accident. *(A quick beat.)* She died.

VIVIAN: You speak of it quite dispassionately. Have you no feelings about what happened?

DRAKE: *(Trying to hide behind a more formal tone:)* If I were still human, maybe. But since my mother and I both ceased to exist that day, it no longer has any meaning for me. It just happened, that's all.

VIVIAN: Ah yes, your resurrection. How did that happen?

DRAKE: My mother and I were in the car for a long time before anyone found us. I was trapped and couldn't help her and she died. *(A small beat.)* And as I lay there looking at her, I felt my spirit leave my body and...I died too.

VIVIAN: *(Looking up from her notes:)* Wait. You actually believe you died?

DRAKE: Sure. How else could I have become undead if I didn't die first? I woke up to a pain in my neck and this guy bending over me.

VIVIAN: The EMT...?

DRAKE: Yeah. He was a vampire. He must've been very old to be able to survive in the daylight like that. He was covered in blood. He was too late to feed on my mother, but not me. I don't know if he meant to turn me or if he just didn't have time to drain me completely, but when I woke up in the hospital, I was like this.

VIVIAN: A vampire.

DRAKE: A monster. *(A beat. He starts again slowly, somewhat embarrassed.)* They thought I was crazy. Talked my dad into letting them keep me. For psychiatric observation, they said. For my own good, they said. So I wouldn't hurt myself. Hmph. They should be so lucky.

VIVIAN: Your father was trying to help you.

DRAKE: Help me? By tying me to the bed? They tied me to the bed!

VIVIAN: They were afraid you'd hurt yourself. Or someone else. You did threaten that nurse, after all.

DRAKE: I didn't threaten her, I warned her! New vampires can't control their hunger and there she was, leaning over me and wiping my brow and acting like—I was afraid I'd attack her and feed off her without knowing what I was doing!

VIVIAN: Well, that's not how she took it. You frightened her badly.

(Drake says nothing.)

How do you feel about that? About scaring her that way?

DRAKE: I don't feel anything. I'm as dead on the inside as I am on the outside.

VIVIAN: And you believe your mother's death was your fault?

DRAKE: Yes.

VIVIAN: Completely and one hundred per cent?

DRAKE: Yes.

VIVIAN: What about the other driver?

DRAKE: What? What does the other driver have to do with anything?

VIVIAN: Don't you feel like he might be partially to blame as well?

DRAKE: *(Stammering:)* No! He just—I mean, it isn't— *(He turns his back to her and crosses to the window)* You're just trying to confuse me.

(Vivian stands and picks up her purse and briefcase.)

VIVIAN: You said earlier that it does not matter what we believe. I disagree. I think it matters a great deal.

(She takes several steps toward him as he keeps looking doggedly at the window.)

Do you want to know what I believe? I believe you're frightened. I believe you're grieving and I believe you're in a tremendous amount of pain. I do not, however, believe you to be some mythological creature of the night and I don't believe that you are in any way responsible for your mother's death.

(She walks to the door, stops and turns back to face him.)

But I do believe I can help you, Drake. And when you're ready, we have a great deal to talk about.

(As she opens the door, the lights on Drake's room go out. Rather than go through the door, she crosses downstage in a straight line to be met by Michael, entering from SL.)

MICHAEL: So, how did it go? Did you find out anything...useful?

VIVIAN: *(Thoughtfully:)* Yes, I did.

MICHAEL: And do you know how to help him?

VIVIAN: *(Turning to face him:)* I know many things, Mr. Prescott. But it does not matter what I know. What matters is what Drake knows, and what he is willing to admit, and to accept. We have much work.

(They begin exiting SL.)

When can I see him again?

(They adlib out.)

SCENE 4

(As Vivian crosses downstage at the end of the last Scene, the middle curtain closes on the bedroom and the cemetery set is moved in on wheeled platforms, complete with trees and tombstones and the front of a large mausoleum at far SL. Additional trees and plants and headstones and fog can be added as desired and as your budget allows. As Vivian and Michael exit, the set change continues and AMANDA CLAYPOOL and PENELOPE WINKLE enter SL. Amanda is clearly in charge and is carrying a tape gun while Penelope is staggering under the load of several reams of fliers advertising the Celebration of Positivity and Goodwill. They enter talking, making a beeline for SR, as Amanda takes one flier after another off Penelope's stack and tapes them up on the set.)

AMANDA: *(Taping up a flier:)* I'm telling you, Penelope, this charity/do-gooder crap is just what I need to get the good schools to notice me. The scholarship committees love this stuff!

PENELOPE: *(Dropping fliers and trying to pick them back up again:)* I'm sure they do, ma'am. But why do you need a scholarship anyway? Aren't you, well, rich?

AMANDA: You're darn right I'm rich! But Daddy is still mad over my wrecking the Porsche and he says he's deducting the price of the car...and the garage...and that tree...from the money for my tuition until I pay it back. That's a lot of money, Penelope! I can't possibly pay it, so I need—

PENELOPE: *(Interrupting:)* A scholarship, ma'am, I get it, but creating a fake charity that doesn't really do anything just to get a scholarship; isn't that kind of, well, cheating?

AMANDA: *(Turning to face her:)* No! My daddy does it with his advertising clients all the time. Get caught using underage slave labor in a Third World country to make your product?

Build a school! Pollute the river by your factory so badly that all the fish have third eyes? Start a foundation! Fund a dictator who oppresses his people by the thousands just to get a bigger mark-up on toothpaste? Invest a —

PENELOPE: *(Interrupting:)* I think I get it now, ma'am. Thank you. And it is very clever. But isn't this whole thing, well, sort of...illegal?

AMANDA: Illegal? This isn't illegal, it's promotional! Do you know what my Daddy calls free enterprise? He says, *"Free enterprise is being able to sell anything you want as long as you don't get caught."* Well, we're selling something, all right. We're selling the idea that I, Amanda Isabella Claypool, am an outstanding scholar—

PENELOPE: You have a "C" average.

AMANDA: —an inspirational leader—

PENELOPE: You slept through the Leadership class at school and when we were in Girl Scouts, you ate all the cookies!

AMANDA: —and a wonderful friend!

PENELOPE: You pay me to hang out with you!

AMANDA: Which makes you an employee, not a friend. Look, if I was already all these things I wouldn't need to sell it, would I? My charity is merely a distraction—

PENELOPE: *(Interrupting:)* Sort of like the shiny, expensive wrapping paper that keeps everyone from noticing that the gift itself is broken?

AMANDA: Well, I don't know that I'd put it like that!

PENELOPE: *(Holding up the flier and reading aloud:)* "A Celebration of Positivity and Goodwill." What does that even mean?

AMANDA: *(Snatching the flier out of Penelope's hand and taping it up:)* It means, Penelope, it means I am *positive* that someone will hear about this and show me some *good will* by offering me a full ride to the college or university of my choice! Now, come on— *(Crossing SR:)* I want to stick the rest of these up before sundown. Move it, sister! Hut two, three, four...

(She exits SR.)

PENELOPE: *(Muttering under her breath as she follows Amanda off, dropping and picking up fliers as she goes:)* I'll tell you where I'd like to stick the rest of these things...

AMANDA: *(Yelling from offstage:)* What was that?

PENELOPE: Nothing, ma'am! Just thinking about places where the sun doesn't shine!

(As Penelope exits SR, the Agents of GEEK enter from SL, dressed as we saw them before.)

DR. FUNK: *(Crossing DC:)* Alright, everyone! Fan out and begin scanning! If we're going to get any evidence of ectoplasmic entropization tonight, the cemetery should be the perfect place for it.

(He adopts a melodramatic pose and lowers his voice as the others take out a variety of bizarre tools and wave them about.)

It was a dark and stormy night. With a chill wind; the kind a cheap novelist would call "laughing..." Bwa-ha-ha...

TOMMY: It's not really all that stormy.

BIT GIRL: More foggy than anything else.

WHINER: Humid. The "air you can wear."

BIT GIRL: *(Giggling; getting a bit silly:)* The air you can wear that's fun to wear!

(Tommy, Bit Girl and Whiner laugh as Dr. Funk shushes them angrily.)

DR. FUNK: Would you three morons shut up? We have work to do! Howling Tommy, you getting any readings?

TOMMY: *(Holding up his monitor and waving it about:)* Negatory, Boss.

BIT GIRL: Hey Whiner, you wanna know why cemeteries are so popular?

WHINER: Why?

BIT GIRL: 'Cause everybody's just *dying* to get in! Get it? Dying?

(Bit Girl and Whiner laugh. By this point, the set change should be finished and Drake will step out quietly in the dark to sit on the steps of the mausoleum.)

DR. FUNK: Would you shut up? *(He checks his instruments and frowns.)* There's nothing happening here. Come on, let's go canvas Grid Two Point Five...

TOMMY: Which one is that?

DR. FUNK: *(Exasperated:)* The one over by the tall bushes! *(Exiting quickly SL:)* I gotta pee!

(He exits and the others follow. Whiner, as usual, goes the wrong way, moving off SR, until she sees a ghostly figure appear from behind the mausoleum. She squeals and runs off SL to join the others.)

(That "ghostly figure" is WYSTERIA, aka AIMEE STRINGER, a melancholy young woman wearing a floor-length antique Victorian-looking dress with plenty of lace and ruffles and a long hooded cape. She enters slowly, not seeing Drake by the mausoleum, and while contemplating a small bunch of

wildflowers she holds in her hands, makes her way just right of Center. Drake watches her as she walks.)

WYSTERIA: *(Reciting from "Echo" by Christina Rossetti, 1830-1894:)* "Yet come to me in dreams, that I may live
My very life again tho' cold in death;
Come back to me in dreams, that I may give
Pulse for pulse, breath for breath;
Speak low, lean low,
As long ago, my love, how long ago."

DRAKE: That's very pretty.

(He startles her and she jumps.)

WYSTERIA: Oh! I didn't see you there! *(She catches her breath.)* Thank you. I didn't write it, though. It's something we read in school.

DRAKE: I especially liked the part where the guy feeds off her dreams so that he can live even though he's stone-cold dead. Cool. Like a zombie.

WYSTERIA: That's not exactly what it says...

DRAKE: I'm Drake. What's your name?

WYSTERIA: *(Draws herself up and assumes a faintly dramatic pose:)* My name is Wysteria Belladonna Nightshade.

DRAKE: *(Incredulously:)* Seriously?

WYSTERIA: Yes, seriously. It is a name given to me by my spirit guide and speaks to the power and mystery of the night and the Earth itself. Unlike Aimee, the name given to me by my parents, which speaks to the bone-crushing dreariness and soul-shattering despair that is my family.

DRAKE: I don't know what that means.

WYSTERIA: It means I hate my life.

DRAKE: Oh! Why didn't you say so? I totally get that! My life sucks too.

WYSTERIA: Wait a minute. Drake. I know you! You're Drake Prescott, the kid who—

(She stops, not sure how to finish.)

DRAKE: Yeah, "the kid who" killed his mother, thinks he's a vampire, may never kiss a girl; take your pick.

WYSTERIA: *(Crossing to him:)* Oh my god, this is so exciting!

DRAKE: *(Warily:)* Really? You're not scared? Or disgusted?

WYSTERIA: Not at all! It's so seldom I get to meet a fellow "creature of the night."

DRAKE: A fellow creature? What are you? *(He looks her over carefully.)* Some kind of witch?

WYSTERIA: No, nothing so outlandish as all that! I am merely a nocturnal spiritualist, a loving child of Gaea, tuned into the rhythm of the tides and the beating of her heart. *(Conspiratorially:)* Confidentially, I did want to be a witch once. A Wiccan, you know? I read all the literature, looked up all the websites and I was all set to sign up-and then I found out what "*skyclad*" meant. I'm sorry, I'm all for communing with Mother Nature and empowering my womanhood and all that, but I am so not dancing naked in the moonlight, not for anyone!

DRAKE: *(Thoroughly confused:)* I don't...blame you?

WYSTERIA: So now I just wear the clothes and drink my tea and commune with my crystals and celebrate the Earth, our Mother in my own inimitable way.

DRAKE: Right...

WYSTERIA: And I write poetry! Would you like to hear one of my poems?

DRAKE: Um, I guess.

(Wysteria draws herself up straight and holds out one hand as if she is addressing a large crowd.)

WYSTERIA: *(Reciting*:)* "I stand inside an empty tomb, this silent coffin of my room.
I watch the people passing there;
see them gaze and see them stare.
They disappear in clouds of incense;
and like the grave, I am...in Silence."

[*There's nothing literate about this one at all. I wrote it when I was fifteen. Have fun.]

(She closes her eyes and bows dramatically.)

DRAKE: *(Not sure what to say:)* Wow. That's...depressing. Good, but depressing.

WYSTERIA: I know, right? I call it a true, honest unburdening of the soul!

DRAKE: What does everyone else call it?

WYSTERIA: A cry for help. But like I told my mother, you only need help when you hold the darkness inside! Once you let it out, you have nothing to fear from it ever again!

DRAKE: Is that true?

WYSTERIA: Sure! Why wouldn't it be? Now tell me, what's it like to be a vampire?

DRAKE: *(Embarrassed:)* I don't know, I'm only just getting started. I'm not very good at it yet.

WYSTERIA: Well, do you drink blood?

DRAKE: No, not until I complete my transformation. Until then, I drink tomato juice, you know, for practice.

WYSTERIA: That's a great idea! You sound like you've really got a handle on this...

> *(Wysteria is interrupted as The Agents of GEEK enter once again from SL. As Dr. Funk begins speaking, however, Wysteria doesn't realize they are there and she and Drake shift their conversation into pantomime.)*

DR. FUNK: *(Entering:)* I don't believe you people! Here I am, trying to establish a new beachhead in the field of paranormal research and investigation and all you want to do is complain!

WHINER: Well, my feet hurt!

TOMMY: And I'm hungry!

DR. FUNK: *(Seeing Wysteria and Drake and hiding behind the mausoleum:)* Hey! We've got company! Bit Girl! Recon and identification!

BIT GIRL: *(Moving to the front and pulling a pair of binoculars out of her bag:)* Gotcha' boss! *(She studies Wysteria and Drake through her binoculars.)* Hmmm...very interesting...very interesting indeed...

DR. FUNK: *(Exasperatedly:)* Would you quit mumbling and tell us who the heck they are?

BIT GIRL: Sorry! The girl is Aimee Stringbean, I mean, Aimee Stringer. She's this weird Goth chick who was in my chem class last year. As for the guy...

> *(She picks up the binoculars and looks at Drake through them again.)*

DR. FUNK: Yes, Bit Girl? You were saying? "As for the guy...?"

BIT GIRL: Well, I'm not a hundred percent, but I think that's the vampire kid.

DR. FUNK: *(Flabbergasted:)* What vampire kid?

TOMMY: Oh, I hearda him! He's the kid that was in that car wreck with his mom and said it turned him into a vampire!

WHINER: How can a car wreck turn you into a vampire?

DR. FUNK: How is there evidence of a real live undead vampire among us and none of you thought to tell me about it?

TOMMY: Why should you care, boss? All you've ever been interested in before is ghosts. Why would you want to know about a vampire?

DR. FUNK: I am interested in any and all proof of the supernatural, Howling Tommy! And a vampire would certainly qualify, now wouldn't it?

(He looks back at Wysteria and Drake and sees Wysteria lift her wrist up to Drake who leans over and sniffs it.)

Wait! What's he doing? Is he biting her? She must be his Renfield!

BIT GIRL: His what?

DR. FUNK: His Renfield! A supernatural servant, bound in slavery to his undead desires! *(In his excitement, he gets louder until he's almost shouting.)* He must have to drink regularly of her blood to keep her under his power!

DRAKE: *(Hearing Dr. Funk shout:)* Did you hear something?

WYSTERIA: *(Looking around:)* No, probably just a cat caught in the bushes. *(Holding her wrist back up:)* So, do you like my perfume? It's lilac.

DRAKE: *(Taking her wrist and sniffing it again:)* Yeah, it's pretty. Kinda' reminds me of my mom.

(Wysteria takes her arm back and there is a quiet beat in honor of Drake's mother.)

WYSTERIA: *(Changing the subject:)* So, you never answered my question. Do you want to go to the movies with me on Friday, or what? It's a double feature, *Wuthering Heights* and *Bleak House*.

DRAKE: Sure. Sounds...fun.

(Wysteria laughs and hugs Drake; a hug which is over before he even gets his arms up. She takes him by the arm and they exit through the cemetery SR. As they exit, the Geeks should emerge from behind the mausoleum and once they clear the curtain line, the curtain should close, allowing the set to be changed for Scene 5.)

DR. FUNK: *(Crossing DC, crowing triumphantly:)* Did you hear that? First he drank her blood and then they sealed their fiendish pact with plans for a sinister social ritual! It's perfect!

BIT GIRL: Since when is a movie sinister?

TOMMY: Maybe he has to buy the popcorn.

WHINER: That doesn't make it sinister, doofus! That makes it a date. Ooh, do you think they're dating? How exciting!

BIT GIRL: And besides, I don't really think he drank her blood, Billy. It looked like he was just smelling her.

WHINER: Gross. When I was in sixth grade, Chris Mueller used to smell all the girls. It was creepy.

DR. FUNK: *(Not listening:)* This is it! The culmination of everything I've ever dreamed of! Everything we've worked for! We shall capture this vampire and force him to give up his secrets and then, for the first time, we shall *know!* Come on, Howling Tommy! We have to buy garlic! Lots of garlic!

(Dr. Funk and Howling Tommy exit SL while Bit Girl and Whiner stay behind.)

BIT GIRL: *(Turning out to speak to the audience:)* I guess, since we're supposed to be providing you with all this extra information, we should take a moment to give you the scoop on Billy...ah, I mean, Dr. Funk.

WHINER: He's crazy.

BIT GIRL: No! Well, yeah, kinda'. But it's understandable. See, when Billy was a kid, he had a little sister.

WHINER: Melody.

BIT GIRL: Right, Melody. And Billy loved her something fierce. And when Melody was three, she got sick. And it was bad. So bad, in fact, they had to put her in the hospital and...she died.

WHINER: *(Sadly, shaking her head:)* Three years old.

BIT GIRL: I know, right? Anyway, Billy was about six at the time and he kept asking people what happens when we die. He got all kinds of answers from all kinds of people, but every time he asked them to prove it, they couldn't. Made him crazy.

WHINER: When I met him in second grade, he was a pretty quiet kid. Unhappy. And angry a lot of the time, too. Like the world had some big secret and nobody would tell him what it was.

BIT GIRL: By the time they taught us how to read, I mean, *really* taught us, Billy took to it in a big way. Pretty soon, he was reading stuff that was way beyond our grade level.

WHINER: *The Hobbit, The Chronicles of Narnia*...and he read the *Harry Potter* books before anybody!

BIT GIRL: Yeah, but that's not all. Anything about the occult or the supernatural, he'd just devour it. Especially if it was about ghosts. Anything about ghosts or the hereafter, he just couldn't get enough of it. And then after books, it was movies and TV shows —

WHINER: And, before you knew it, The Agents of GEEK was born.

BIT GIRL: Mostly, we just sit around and watch movies or read comics or play video games. And when we do go out, it's like *larping*, you know? Live Action Role Playing? We dress up in— *(Indicating their clothes:)* —silly costumes and call each other by goofy names and pretend we're the Ghostbusters or something.

WHINER: Except for Billy.

BIT GIRL: Right. For Billy, it's serious business. He really wants to know if there's a Heaven or a Nirvana or a Valhalla, so he can know that his little sister is OK somewhere. He can get pretty intense about it.

WHINER: Like that time at the Fair.

BIT GIRL: Oh god, The Pennsylvania State Fair. We were just out having a good time, right? We weren't even in uniform; just scarfing down popcorn and cotton candy and riding the Tilt-a-Whirl 'til we were about to throw up, when Billy noticed a fortune teller's booth on the Midway, and suddenly, he just had to have his fortune told.

WHINER: We told him it was fake.

BIT GIRL: Of course, we told him it was fake! He knew it was fake! But he gave us that look he gets, you know, the one that says he knows everything and we know nothing?

WHINER: Boy, do I know that look.

BIT GIRL: And he told us that, just like that magic fortune telling machine in *Big*—you know, the Tom Hanks movie—the world sometimes tucks real magic away in the most ordinary places and how were we going to know until we checked? So off he went, and of course, we followed.

WHINER: Well, Tommy would follow Billy anywhere.

BIT GIRL: That's true. Tommy is Billy's best friend and enforcer and if Billy told him to take a flying leap, the only thing Tommy would ask is "how high," but we went too. It was like a train wreck. You know it's gonna be a disaster, but you just can't look away.

WHINER: If the fortune teller really had any talent in the first place, she'd have seen it coming.

BIT GIRL: Anyway, Billy went in, but the fortune teller made the rest of us wait outside. A couple of minutes later, we heard Billy cry out and there was a crash and then all hell broke loose.

WHINER: She tried to fool him.

BIT GIRL: Yeah, you know how those fortunetellers work, right? They start chatting you up before the reading starts to get some sense of why you're there and what you're looking for? Well, Billy knew better and didn't give her anything and so when she began the reading, she was flying blind.

WHINER: The blind leading the blind.

BIT GIRL: She'd ask him all these leading questions and he'd just say, "I don't know. You're the fortune teller, you tell me," so finally, she went off on some crazy story about some girl he liked liking him back. I guess she figured Billy must be sweet on one of us.

WHINER: As if!

BIT GIRL: Once Billy realized she was a fake, he just lost it. He kicked over her table and ripped up her Tarot cards and stomped on her candles. By the time we got in there and started trying to hold him down, he'd ripped a couple tapestries off the wall and the fortune teller had a black eye.

WHINER: And that's when the cops got there.

BIT GIRL: Yeah. The black eye made it assault, so Billy got arrested. But once the fortune teller realized she'd have to go to the station and make a statement, she changed her tune and refused to press charges. We found out later that she had a couple of outstanding warrants in New York for petty theft that she apparently didn't want the cops to know about.

WHINER: Saved by the fact that she was an even bigger criminal than we were!

BIT GIRL: And so that's Billy, better known as Dr. Megatron Von Funkenstein, buster of ghosts, vanquisher of fortunetellers, vampire slayer, astral projectionist—

WHINER: And still a six-year-old kid at heart, whose sister died without telling him why.

BIT GIRL: And he still gets angry. So very, very angry. And I have a real "fortune teller feeling" about this vampire kid. Like there's another train coming—

WHINER: And once again, we won't be able to get out of the way.

DR. FUNK: *(Off:)* Bit Girl! Whiner! Are you coming?

BIT GIRL: *(To Whiner:)* That's our cue. *(Back to audience:)* So, look, whatever happens, don't hate Billy too much, OK? He's just lost.

WHINER: Just like the rest of us. Hey, Cheryl?

BIT GIRL: Yeah, Dawn?

WHINER: What do *you* think happens to us when we die?

BIT GIRL: Oh, that's easy. Rainbows.

WHINER: Huh?

BIT GIRL: Sure. Rainbows and unicorns and chocolate ice cream sundaes, every day of the week.

WHINER: Really? Cool.

(She races off SL to join Dr. Funk and Tommy.)

BIT GIRL: *(Watches her leave, then turns back to audience.)* What can I tell you? Everybody's gotta believe in something.

(She exits SL.)

SCENE 5

(As Bit Girl exits, the curtain opens just enough to push Drake's front door in, as in Scene 1. Vivian enters, walking briskly as always. Michael comes out on the porch to meet her.)

MICHAEL: Ah, Dr. Marquette. There you are.

(She stops and looks up at him.)

VIVIAN: Another clandestine front porch rendezvous, Michael? We have to stop meeting like this.

MICHAEL: What?

VIVIAN: Nothing. What's wrong? Where's Drake?

MICHAEL: I don't know. He's not here.

VIVIAN: Not here? I thought he refused to leave his bedroom?

MICHAEL: He did. He does! But lately he's been leaving every night just after dark and not coming home until after midnight. I'm worried.

VIVIAN: Yes, I can see that.

(She walks up the steps, on to the porch.)

Let's go inside. You can pour me a cup of tea and tell me more about your son's late-night wandering.

(They exit through front door, just as Drake and Wysteria enter in the middle of a friendly conversation.)

DRAKE: *(Awkwardly:)* So, thanks for coming over to my house this time.

WYSTERIA: Not a problem. I was wondering what it looked like. *(She turns to him excitedly.)* Do you have a coffin?

DRAKE: No. Just a bed. Sometimes, I close myself up in the closet, though, and that feels like a coffin, sort of. At least it's dark, though I don't imagine most coffins smell of mothballs and fabric softener. I can show it to you later, if you want.

WYSTERIA: That'd be great. And this is your yard?

DRAKE: This is it. A sprinkler, some crab grass and some dried dog poop you'll find later if you're not careful. We spared no expense.

WYSTERIA: *(Hopefully:)* I don't suppose you were—

DRAKE: *(Finishing her sentence:)* —Buried here? No. I did have a parakeet once that lost an argument with Mrs. Berkley's cat. It's buried over there under that planter. So far, it hasn't risen from the dead, though. Only me. *(An awkward pause.)* So...how was school today?

(Wysteria sits.)

WYSTERIA: BOR-ing! I swear, if I ever use Algebra in real life, I will come back and pay Mrs. Sheffield a million dollars. I did write a new poem, though. Would you like to hear it?

DRAKE: Sure.

(Wysteria takes a folded up piece of paper out of her pocket and stands, resuming her more formal pose from the cemetery.)

WYSTERIA: *(Reciting from "She Walks in Beauty" by Lord Byron:)* "She walks in beauty, like the night
Of cloudless climes and starry skies,
Let Tommy Spencer fall within my sight,
That I might strike him, between the eyes."

DRAKE: What?

WYSTERIA: What?

DRAKE: It's just, in my head I saw that going in a totally different direction.

WYSTERIA: It's a work in progress, now shush! *(She returns to her formal pose again and continues her recitation.)* "And as he falls and falls away,
Perhaps he'll think about that day,
When he refused to take me to the prom,
And lost his wits upon the...upon...oh, it's no use. I can't think of a rhyme for "prom!"

DRAKE: What if you use "dance" instead? *(He adopts a weak caricature of Wysteria's pose.)* "When he refused to take me to the dance,
And I was forced to kick him, in the pants."
How's that?

(She takes out a pencil and begins scratching something out on her paper.)

WYSTERIA: I like it!

(She starts to write, but then her shoulders slump and she begins crossing things out again.)

No, it sucks! It all sucks! *(Crossing to Drake:)* Oh Drake, you have no idea how lucky you are!

DRAKE: Lucky? Me?

WYSTERIA: Of course! You have no idea what it's like to be ordinary and live a boring normal life! I live in a perfect house with a perfect yard with a perfect little brother and a perfect dog—

DRAKE: I like dogs. They don't like me, though. My Aunt Sadie had a Schnauzer once and all it ever wanted to do was chew up my socks and try to pee on my leg.

WYSTERIA: Well, I have the perfect dog, who always goes on the paper, never slobbers on the shoes, never chases the mailman—he's even got the perfect name—Chipper. Who names a dog Chipper? I swear my life is so dull it makes reruns of *Full House* look like *Masterpiece Theatre*!

DRAKE: I like the name Chipper...

WYSTERIA: And I haven't even told you the worst part yet.

DRAKE: There's a "worst" part?

WYSTERIA: You have no idea! *(Looking around carefully:)* I'll tell you this, Drake, but you have to swear you'll never tell anyone!

DRAKE: My god, what happened?

WYSTERIA: Do you swear?

DRAKE: I swear, I swear! May my life go straight to hell in a handbasket if I ever tell—oh, wait, that happened already. Well, I still swear—

(He locks his lips and throws away the key.)

Your secret's safe with me.

WYSTERIA: Are you ready?

DRAKE: I'm ready.

WYSTERIA: I can't believe I'm telling you this.

DRAKE: Me either, because so far, you haven't told me anything!

WYSTERIA: This is so embarrassing!

DRAKE: Wysteria! In 12 hours the sun will come up and I'll burn to death, all because I'm still standing here, waiting for you to let me in on this big secret. *That* will be embarrassing! This is merely pointless.

WYSTERIA: I don't know...

DRAKE: Wysteria! Tell me!

AIMEE: *(Shouting;)* My parents have a happy marriage!

DRAKE: *(Incredulous:)* What?

WYSTERIA: They don't fight, they don't get mad—any other house would be filled with all sorts of delicious family drama! Will their marriage survive? Will one of them have an affair? Will they manage to keep it all together for the sake of the kids? You know how in some families the parents close the door so the kids won't hear them fighting?

DRAKE: Yeah.

WYSTERIA: Not mine! My parents close the door because they can't keep their hands off each other! At their age! My dad is almost 50, for crying out loud!

DRAKE: It sounds sweet...

WYSTERIA: Sweet? Drake, you don't know how good you have it. You get to live your life in a cocoon of such pain and anguish. A wonderful symphony of feeling and heartbreak that most of us have never known. It's exquisite!

DRAKE: It is?

WYSTERIA: Of course! Drake, the things that have happened to you are so deep; so real! You dance every day on such a fault line of despair and self-destruction, it gives me goose bumps just thinking about it. I'd give anything to feel that powerful! To feel that alive!

DRAKE: Wysteria. Wait a minute. You wish you had a life like mine? My life sucks. My mom is dead and I'm the one who killed her. I'm a monster! My dad is so depressed he can barely get out of bed in the morning and you're worried that your dog won't chase the mailman? Any day, I'm afraid I'm gonna chase the mailman and take a big hunk out of his neck! I hate my life.

WYSTERIA: Drake, I didn't mean —

DRAKE: *(Interrupting her:)* My parents used to be happy. They held hands and laughed, and then I killed it and no one will ever laugh in this house again. *(A beat as he turns to look at her.)* I thought you got it. I thought you understood what I was going through.

(She runs to him and gives him a tight hug, but he doesn't respond.)

WYSTERIA: I'm so stupid! I do get it, Drake. I really do! It's just that my own life is so bloody pointless! *(Stepping away from him in frustration:)* Sometimes I get so tired of being ordinary that I could just scream!

DRAKE: Ordinary? I think you're amazing.

(Michael comes through front door.)

MICHAEL: Drake! You need to come in now. Your guest is here.

(Michael exits back into the house.)

DRAKE: My "guest." Look at him; he's so ashamed of me that he can't even admit I'm in therapy. I guess I'd better go.

WYSTERIA: OK. Oh, I brought you a present!

DRAKE: Really?

(She pulls a beat-up old hardback book out of her bag and hands it to him.)

WYSTERIA: I saw it in the used bookstore today and thought you might like it.

DRAKE: *(Looking at the cover:)* John Polly— Poli...

WYSTERIA: John Polidori. It's pretty old. The story, I mean. The first one of its kind. There's a foreword inside if you want to read it. Anyway— *(An awkward pause.)* Enjoy your therapy.

DRAKE: Thanks. How do my eyes look? I don't want to go in there with bloodshot eyes.

WYSTERIA: *(Looking closely at his eyes:)* I told you that you were drinking too much tomato juice.

DRAKE: Yeah. You headed back to your perfect home?

WYSTERIA: *(Smiling awkwardly:)* I guess. Are you still going to come to the movies with me tonight?

DRAKE: That's tonight? Oh jeez, Wysteria, I don't know—

WYSTERIA: Please? I'll buy the popcorn.

DRAKE: Well, in that case. Can we put some "O positive" on it?

WYSTERIA: What?

DRAKE: I'm kidding. I guess I'll see you there.

WYSTERIA: Great.

(She quickly gives him a peck on the cheek and exits.)

Bye! See you tonight!

(Drake just stands there touching his cheek where she kissed him when Michael calls from inside.)

MICHAEL: *(Off:)* Drake? Are you coming, son?

DRAKE: I'm coming, Dad. *(To himself:)* I wonder if Godzilla ever has days like this.

SCENE 6

(As Drake exits into the house, the curtains open to reveal Drake's bedroom, just as Michael and Vivian come through the door.)

MICHAEL: *(A little nervous:)* I'm not sure how Drake is going to feel about you being in here without him.

VIVIAN: It's all a part of the therapeutic process. If I'm to root out the terrors that plague your son's psyche, then I must be allowed full access! We must shake loose the cobwebs! Beat the rugs! Take out the trash!

MICHAEL: You really like cleaning, huh?

VIVIAN: *(A little embarrassed:)* Huh? Oh, well, yes. I'm a little obsessive about it. Sorry. We all have our issues, eh?

MICHAEL: Hey, "cleanliness is next to godliness," right?

VIVIAN: Actually, no. The word before "cleanliness" in most dictionaries is "clean-limbed." And the word after is "clean-living."

MICHAEL: Well, I think it means—

(He is interrupted by Drake coming through the door with the book from Wysteria in his hand.)

DRAKE: *(Crossing to them angrily:)* Hey, what are you guys doing in my room?

(He begins moving around the room, checking various hiding places for important items. As he searches, he tosses the book on the bed.)

Haven't you people ever heard of privacy?

VIVIAN: Of course, we have, Drake. But surely you know as a 14-year-old boy, you are not entitled to privacy unless your father says so. It is, after all, his house.

DRAKE: *(Still searching:)* I thought it was "our" house. *(Sullenly, under his breath:)* It was when Mom was alive.

VIVIAN: Indeed. Your father has told me that your mother was the glue that held you all together. Why don't we talk about that? *(Turning to Michael:)* If you'll excuse us?

(She pushes him toward the door.)

MICHAEL: I'm sorry he got so upset, but I told you we shouldn't be in here.

VIVIAN: *(Finally getting him out the door:)* Nonsense. We're establishing boundaries. Besides, thanks to Drake, the next time we're here, we now know all the good places to look.

(Drake stops searching, embarrassed that he's been fooled, as Vivian closes the door in Michael's face.)

(Turning back to Drake:) There. I thought he'd never leave.

(She pulls the chair out from Drake's desk and sits.)

Now we can talk.

(Drake flops down on the bed and lies back, opening the book he brought in and leafing through it.)

DRAKE: *(Disinterested:)* It's your nickel.

VIVIAN: Actually, it is *your* nickel, Drake, or rather, your father's. And quite a bit more than one besides, so let's make the most of them, shall we? *(A beat.)* Where were you?

DRAKE: What?

VIVIAN: You weren't here when I arrived. Where were you?

DRAKE: Out in the yard, if it's any of your business.

VIVIAN: Isn't that dangerous for you?

DRAKE: Not if the sun's gone down. Then it's just dangerous for other people.

VIVIAN: And was the sun down when you went into the backyard?

DRAKE: *(Sitting up:)* Well, duh! I'm here, aren't I? If I'd gone outside while the sun was still up, I'd have spontaneously combusted, now wouldn't I? Ipso facto, if I'm still here, it must have been dark.

VIVIAN: Forgive me. I am still not quite conversant in all the rules of your affliction. Ipso facto. *(Another beat.)* Your father tells me you've been going out quite a bit lately, usually until midnight or later. Where do you go?

DRAKE: *(Looking away:)* The cemetery.

VIVIAN: Really? Are you looking for fresh brains to eat?

DRAKE: No! That's zombies! Jeez, you really don't know anything, do you?

(She stands and crosses to him.)

VIVIAN: I know enough to know that you are not haunting the cemetery alone. Who are you meeting there?

DRAKE: *(Guardedly:)* Who told you that I'm meeting somebody?

VIVIAN: You did. If you were merely languishing amongst the tombstones, you might go out once or twice a week. But every night? No, there is something specific you do in the graveyard; something you look forward to.

DRAKE: *(Standing:)* Maybe I'm just visiting my mom.

VIVIAN: Perhaps. I'm sure you are. But then, there is the matter of this book.

(She crosses to the bed, picking up the book given to him by Wysteria.)

There is a great deal of reading material in this room. Comic books, magazines, paperbacks; all very disposable, to be thrown away when you're finished with them. But this book is a hardcover, and an old one at that. It doesn't fit. What did Big Bird used to say? "One of these things is not like the other"? Ergo, someone gave it to you. And since no one has come here to visit you, it must be someone you visit with on your nocturnal travels. Someone you meet in the cemetery. Ha, I am like Sherlock Holmes, no? Elementary, yes? Ipso facto?

DRAKE: Right. Elementary. You're very clever.

VIVIAN: *(Looking at the cover of the book)* Hmm, what have we here? *(Drake tries to snatch the book away from her, but is unsuccessful:)* The Vampyre by John Polidori.

DRAKE: It's like, one of the very first vampire stories ever! Written way back in 1818.

VIVIAN: And who told you this?

(Drake looks away, embarrassed that he's been caught.)

Come, come, Drake. You can trust me. Who gave you the book?

DRAKE: *(Reluctantly:)* A friend.

VIVIAN: What friend? A ghost? Another vampire? Some mugwump that lives under a headstone?

DRAKE: A what? No! *(Suddenly shy:)* She's a girl. Her name is Wysteria.

VIVIAN: Wysteria? That doesn't sound like a real name. Are you sure this isn't some imaginary friend?

DRAKE: She's as real as you are!

VIVIAN: Alright, alright. I am convinced. And why did she give you this book? Does she think she's a vampire, too? Was she bitten by some over-sexed football player in shoulder pads and an opera cape?

DRAKE: *(Taking the book back:)* No, she just prefers the night, that's all. She gave me the book because she thought it might help if I knew my history.

VIVIAN: Ah. And what else does this Wysteria help you with?

DRAKE: What do you mean?

VIVIAN: I mean, what do you do together? Do you track down virgins for a midnight snack? Howl at the moon? What?

DRAKE: She just reads me poetry. And she invited me to the movies tonight.

VIVIAN: *(Sitting down:)* Poetry. Hmmm. And are you going to go?

DRAKE: Go where?

VIVIAN: To the movies! Your father and I have been trying to get you to leave this house and have some fun for a month now and suddenly, this mere slip of a girl comes along and with one invitation has you considering a wild night on the town! Are you going to go?

DRAKE: It's not a wild night on the town, it's just a movie. And besides, it's not like I can go.

VIVIAN: Really? Why not?

DRAKE: *(He begins pacing anxiously.)* You know why! Out there, in the world, surrounded by so many people; something could happen!

VIVIAN: Of course, something could happen! You could have a good time!

DRAKE: I could hurt somebody! Even worse, I could kill somebody else.

(She tries to go to him, but he backs away.)

VIVIAN: Drake, you did not kill your mother.

DRAKE: You don't know! You weren't there! Everywhere I go, people keep getting hurt!

VIVIAN: What about Wysteria? Don't you feel safe with her?

DRAKE: Safe? What's safe? Wysteria doesn't threaten me, that's all. Doesn't try to make me be normal or ordinary. She just lets me be.

VIVIAN: And you wouldn't want to hurt her, would you?

DRAKE: Hurt her? You still don't get it! I don't want to hurt anybody, but it's not up to me!

(He turns to her so quickly that it startles her.)

Wysteria has this perfume. She says it smells like lilacs, but do you know what I smell? All I can smell is the blood flowing under her skin. All I can hear is her heart pounding in her chest! When I'm with her I get so confused—!

(Vivian approaches him from behind and tries to guide him back to the chair.)

VIVIAN: But that's all perfectly normal—

DRAKE: No!

(As she touches him, he reacts violently, shoving her away and making her fall to the floor.)

It's *not* normal, don't you get it? I could hurt her! I *will* hurt her! Because I'm a monster and pain and death is what monsters do!

(He cries out and crosses to the door, just as Michael enters.)

MICHAEL: Drake, I heard — what is it, what's wrong?

(Drake pushes past him and exits. Michael sees Vivian sitting on the floor and goes to help her up.)

Vivian! Dr. Marquette, are you OK?

(As Vivian speaks, she and Michael cross DC and the lights go down on the bedroom.)

VIVIAN: It was an accident. Nothing damaged except my pride. *(Straightening her clothing and collecting herself.)* I'm afraid I'm not being very helpful to your son. Every time I think I have led him to a good place; a place of healing and forgiveness, he throws up his walls and retreats back into his midnight movie fantasy that he's a menace to everyone he knows! *(She looks at him.)* Is there anything else about the accident? Anything you haven't told me?

MICHAEL: I've told you everything I know. I don't know what's wrong with him any more than you do.

VIVIAN: Have you noticed that while everyone else calls him a vampire, Drake never uses that word in reference to himself? When he names himself, he always uses the word "monster." As if he is trying to remind us that he is not some tragic figure of Gothic romance, but a mindless beast. A creature. A killer.

MICHAEL: And does that mean something?

VIVIAN: Everything means something. It's my job to figure out what and I'm afraid I'm failing. *(She shakes her head.)* Come. We must find Drake. With the mood he's in, he could hurt himself — or someone else.

(They exit together.)

SCENE 7

(As Vivian and Michael exit, the front curtain closes and a crowd of teenagers fill the apron, most of them standing in line, waiting to buy tickets to a movie. You can use a velvet rope or something similar to illustrate this and some sort of mock-up movie poster for Wuthering Heights *and/or* Bleak House *should be on the wall. Standing out in front of the line are Amanda and Penelope, handing out their fliers to everyone in line. Penelope is mainly apologizing for Amanda's cheerful rudeness. As Amanda begins speaking, The Agents of GEEK enter and watch her work.)*

AMANDA: *(Rudely shoving fliers in people's faces:)* Come one, come all! The First-Ever Celebration of Positivity and Goodwill—

PENELOPE: *(Parroting her:)* Positivity and Goodwill!

AMANDA: —will be held this Saturday in the East Side High School auditorium! Come for the free food and the music—

PENELOPE: —Free food and music!

AMANDA: —and stay for the inspirational speeches!

PENELOPE: The Station of Inspiration!

AMANDA: Find out how you can become the Change you want to see in the world!

PENELOPE: Change back from your dollar!

(Amanda gives her an ugly look.)

What?

(As Amanda forces fliers on people, many of them just let them fall to the ground. Penelope runs around picking them up again, trying to straighten the wrinkles out.)

DR. FUNK: *(Picking a flier up off of the ground:)* Hey, check out Sister Mary Sunshine! What's the cause du jour this time? "Fight for Non-Violence"? "Arrest Injustice"?

(He and the Geeks read the flier.)

AMANDA: Hello everyone! For the record, my name is Amanda Isabella Claypool —

PENELOPE: *(Interrupting:)* And I am Penelope Clementine Winkle!

AMANDA: — and I —

PENELOPE: *(Interrupting again:)* We —

AMANDA: *(Giving Penelope a "knock it off or else" look:)* — Represent The Celebration of Positivity and Goodwill!

PENELOPE: Where there's a Good-will, there's a good way!

AMANDA: *(Handing the entire stack of fliers into the crowd where they are passed out and read:)* Take a flier, people. That's it, there's enough for everyone. Let The Celebration of Positivity and Goodwill lead you to your place in the sun! *(Turning back to Penelope:)* Do you have any hand sanitizer? I think one of those idiots actually touched me. If somebody screwed up my hundred dollar manicure—!

PENELOPE: *(Looking at a flier:)* Ma'am, can I just ask you about this flier for a minute? You've got twelve bands on here, five different big-name celebrities and three professional athletes —

AMANDA: You think we need more athletes? Feel free to write a couple in if you want.

PENELOPE: But that's just it, ma'am. We don't know any of these people! What are we going to do on the day of the Celebration when none of the acts actually show up to perform?

AMANDA: *(She is still shaking hands and handing out fliers:)* Bottom right-hand corner.

PENELOPE: What?

AMANDA: The flier. Look at the bottom right-hand corner.

(She turns away from her admirers and points to the flier.)

See right there, in small print; "Program subject to change without notice." We'll just swap everybody out on the day of the show. It's not my fault the sheep didn't read the fine print!

PENELOPE: But who—?

AMANDA: My daddy's got a whole roster of Self-Help hacks who'll fill the show for free in exchange for one hundred percent of the money they make off their stupid books and CDs. Trust me, I've got this all under control.

PENELOPE: I don't know, ma'am. This sounds like—

DR. FUNK: *(Still looking at the flier, interrupting Penelope:)* — The most ridiculous thing I've ever heard! What on Earth is The Celebration of Positivity and Goodwill?

AMANDA: The Celebration of Positivity and Goodwill is a not for profit charitable organization, not affiliated with any political group or religious organization. We are a non-partisan global belief system that encompasses all faiths, all beliefs and all denominations—

DR. FUNK: Yeah, denominations of fifties, hundreds—

WHINER: *(Interrupting:)* Two hundreds!

DR. FUNK: *(Impatiently, to Whiner:)* Shut up, Whiner! *(Looking back at Amanda and throwing the flier to the ground:)* Just another scam!

AMANDA: We'll have free food and all kinds of free musical entertainment!

DR. FUNK: What kind of music could she get? The Marching Band? The Ladies Aide Glee Club? Justin Beiber?*

*(*Feel free to substitute the name of your least favorite pop star.)*

(Wysteria enters. She is not paying any attention to Amanda or the Geeks, nor is she getting into the ticket line for the movie. She is looking for Drake. She stands looking around with a confused expression.)

WHINER: *(Excitedly:)* Ooh, is Justin Beiber coming?

DR. FUNK: Shut up, Whiner! *(To the Geeks:)* They wanna hear some music? Check this out!

(Dance music begins. Rapping:)

IF YOU'RE LOOKING FOR A WORLD MADE OF SUGAR AND

THE GEEKS: SPICE!

DR. FUNK: WHERE EVERYBODY'S FRIENDLY AND THEY ACT

THE GEEKS: REAL NICE!

DR. FUNK: DON'T GO STEPPIN' ON A

THE GEEKS: CRACK!

DR. FUNK: DON'T WANNA BREAK YO' MAMA'S

THE GEEKS: BACK!

DR. FUNK: IF YOU BELIEVE AMANDA, THEN YOU DON'T KNOW

THE GEEKS: JACK!

(The music ends, the Geeks laugh and the folks in the movie line applaud. Not because they like the Geeks, but because they don't really know what's going on.)

(As the Geeks take their bows and laugh at Amanda, Drake enters SL and crosses to Wysteria.)

AMANDA: Rest assured, everyone! *That* music is not on the agenda!

PENELOPE: I don't know, I kind of liked it.

AMANDA: *(Turning to face Penelope, shocked:)* Penelope!

(As Amanda and Penelope begin fighting soundlessly, Drake taps Wysteria on the shoulder, startling her.)

WYSTERIA: Oh! Drake! You almost scared the life out of me!

DRAKE: *(Sheepishly:)* Sorry. Isn't that what us "creatures of the night" are supposed to do?

WYSTERIA: Very funny. Are you ready to go to the movie?

DRAKE: Well, about that. You see, I don't think—

(Tommy notices Drake and Wysteria.)

TOMMY: *(Pointing at Drake and Wysteria:)* Hey, Boss! Check it out.

DR. FUNK: *(Turning to look:)* Aha! The trap is sprung!

(Dr. Funk begins crossing SL when Amanda notices Drake for the first time and pushes her way past Dr. Funk and the Geeks to get to him first.)

AMANDA: Oh, I know you!

(She rudely pushes past Wysteria and grabs Drake by the arm and brings him back Center, where they are surrounded by the Geeks.)

You're that boy who went crazy from being trapped in that car with his dead mother! You are just the kind of person who could benefit from a little Positivity and Goodwill!

PENELOPE: Feel the benefits!

WYSTERIA: *(Being held back by Tommy:)* Leave him alone!

PENELOPE: *(Whispering to Amanda:)* Ma'am, what are we doing now?

AMANDA: Are you kidding? This is exactly what our so-called Celebration needs, a poster boy!

(She turns to Drake and takes his arm, awkwardly trying to comfort him.)

Now, don't you worry about them, sweetie. You just let Amanda help you to take your frown and turn it upside down—

DRAKE: *(Interrupting her:)* Are you kidding me?

AMANDA: Oh, not at all. The Celebration of Positivity and Goodwill can show you how to take the lemons of your life and turn them into an ocean of lemonade!

PENELOPE: Ocean in motion!

AMANDA: We all know you didn't mean to kill your mother—

(Everyone looks shocked that Amanda would say such a thing.)

DRAKE: What?

BIT GIRL: Oh my god!

PENELOPE: Ma'am, maybe now is not a good time—

AMANDA: —but you have to admit it and turn that tragedy into something positive.

DRAKE: I'm positive you've lost your mind. *(To Dr. Funk:)* Is she crazy?

(Dr. Funk angrily spins Drake around to face him.)

DR. FUNK: Yes, but it doesn't mean she's wrong. Admit it! Did you kill your mother?

DRAKE: What?

DR. FUNK: Are you a vampire?

AMANDA: *(Pulling Drake toward her:)* A vampire? What are you, stupid? Anyone with half a brain can tell all this poor boy needs is some positivity and goodwill—

DR. FUNK: *(Pulling Drake back toward him:)* Positivity? I'm positive you're about to make me angry, Amanda, and believe me, you don't want to make me angry!

TOMMY: *(Interjecting:)* Yeah, you wouldn't like us when we're angry!

DR. FUNK: All this poor boy needs is some sunlight and a half a pound of garlic! Answer the question, Count Drake-ula! Are you a vampire? Is there any reason at all why I shouldn't just shove a wooden stake through your heart right now?

DRAKE: It would hurt?

DR. FUNK: The public has the right to know! *(Chanting:)* Are you a vampire? Are you a vampire?

(The crowd joins the chant.)

EVERYONE: *(Except Wysteria, Drake, Amanda and Bit Girl)* Are you a vampire? Are you a vampire?

(As the chant continues, Dr. Funk and Amanda begin pulling Drake back and forth as he gets more and more upset. Tommy continues to hold Wysteria back and things get ugly.)

DR. FUNK: *(Shouting over the chanting:)* Tell us the truth! What are you hiding from us? Tell us your secrets!

AMANDA: *(Shouting over the chanting:)* Would you just leave this poor boy alone? I can help him! I can lead him to peace and understanding. We can take your lemons and make lemonade!

(This doesn't need to go on for very long, but the intensity of it needs to grow quickly as Drake becomes more and more upset and confused. At the height of the chanting and shoving, Drake strikes out blindly, pushing Dr. Funk away and hitting Amanda in the face, knocking her to the ground.)

DRAKE: *(As he lashes out:)* Leave me alone! I'm a monster!

(The chanting stops in shock at the sudden violence. Wysteria rushes to Drake and Penelope bends down to help Amanda, who is moaning in pain.)

(Drake looks around helplessly and then looks at Wysteria with a heartbroken expression.)

(Softly:) I'm a monster.

(With a sob, he runs off. Wysteria follows him, calling his name.)

WYSTERIA: *(Following him out:)* Drake! Wait for me!

TOMMY: After him!

(He exits, followed by a portion of the crowd. The rest of the Geeks and the remainder of the crowd stay behind.)

AMANDA: *(Struggling to stand:)* Penelope? Penelope, where are you?

PENELOPE: *(Hurrying to Amanda:)* Right here, ma'am! Are you OK? What can I do?

AMANDA: Do, Penelope? Haven't you already done enough? You allowed me to stand next to a crazy person, you let that crazy person strike me in the face, you abandoned me as I lay bleeding—!

(Howling Tommy and his helpers return.)

DR. FUNK: Tommy! Did you get him?

TOMMY: We had him, Boss. And we were kicking the crap out of him pretty good too, when that crazy Goth chick jumped me from behind and he got away. He's pretty hurt, though. I think we can catch him.

(Tommy's group exits again.)

DR. FUNK: *(Addressing the crowd:)* Alright, everyone, we have a dangerous creature on the loose in our fair city and we need to track it down! The Angry Mob will gather at my house in—

AMANDA: *(Pushing Dr. Funk out of the way and holding a cloth to her badly bleeding nose:)* Oh, get out of my way! *(To crowd:)* Attention everyone! I was just attacked and almost killed by a dangerous psychopath who thinks he's a vampire! It is our job—nay, it is our duty—as red, white and blue Americans to track this psycho down and make him pay! Who's with me?

(The crowd roars their approval.)

PENELOPE: Now what are we doing, ma'am? I thought he was going to be our poster boy!

AMANDA: This is even better! I am now the innocent victim at the center of a soon-to-be national manhunt. If we play this right, I'll get on TV and the offers will come pouring in! Every college in America will want me! In fact, forget college! If that kid could manage to get himself killed in a shootout with the police, I bet they'll put me on *Oprah!*

(*Handing Penelope the bloody rag, Amanda exits, followed by the crowd.*)

PENELOPE: (*Holding the rag like it's radioactive and following her out:*) Ma'am, we can't do this! Not only is it wrong, but I don't even think *Oprah's* on any more!

DR. FUNK: (*Trying in vain to lead a crowd that is no longer there:*) OK everybody, bring your own torches and protest signs, and if you want, we can stop by my house — my mom should have cookies if anybody's hungry! Let's go!

(*He moves to exit.*)

WHINER: But Billy, what about —

DR. FUNK: (*Angrily:*) Shut up, Whiner. When I want your opinion, I'll give it to you. Now, come on!

(*He shoves past them, and he and Tommy exit after Drake and Bit Girl tries to pull Whiner after her.*)

WHINER: Anybody else hear a train coming? I do.

(*Bit Girl grabs her again and pulls her off to exit.*)

(*End of Act I.*)

ACT II

SCENE 1

(The main curtain is closed. The Agents of GEEK assemble in the center of the apron for the Act II Opening Rap:)

DR. FUNK: WELL, YOU'VE BEEN LISTENING TO MY STORY 'BOUT A BOY NAMED—

THE GEEKS: DRAKE!

DR. FUNK: HIS LIFE IS FULL OF TROUBLE AND HE CAN'T CATCH A—

THE GEEKS: BREAK!

TOMMY: HE'S DOWN IN THE MUCK!

WHINER: AND HE'S ALL OUTTA' LUCK!

DR. FUNK: LIVING LIKE A VAMPIRE HAS REALLY GOT TO—

THE GEEKS: SUCK!

(Amidst thunderous applause, the Geeks take several bows and high fives and run off, except for Whiner, who doesn't see everyone leave and keeps bowing until Bit Girl comes back out to get her. Embarrassed, Whiner takes one last bow and runs off as Bit Girl looks at the audience.)

BIT GIRL: *(To audience:)* Hey, thanks for coming back. You haven't missed much, really. Just running. Lots and lots of running.

(She takes a small bow and exits.)

SCENE 2

(The curtain opens on the cemetery, looking the same as before. The only time that has passed between Act I and now is the time it took to run from the movie theatre. Drake enters, SL. He has been beaten up and it shows with cuts and bruises on his face. He has also been running and is now extremely out of breath. In fact, the only reason he's stopping is because he physically cannot run anymore. He collapses to the stage, gasping for breath as Wysteria enters behind him. She is also out of breath, but not as badly as Drake.)

WYSTERIA: Drake! You've been hurt. You need a doctor.

DRAKE: *(Still breathing heavily:)* Go away. Leave...me alone.

WYSTERIA: Drake, it was an accident! You didn't mean to hit Amanda. And you're bleeding. What can I do?

(On this last line, Dr. Funk and Bit Girl enter SR. During this next exchange, Dr. Funk and Bit Girl stay on the SR side of the stage, while Drake and Wysteria stay on the SL side. Despite the fact that they appear to be answering one another's questions and finishing one another's sentences, the two couples cannot see one another or hear one another.)

DR. FUNK: What could you do? You could have helped me, Bit Girl! I needed you!

BIT GIRL: Well, I'm sorry, but I was *trying* to help! I was trying to clean up your mess!

DRAKE: My god, what a mess! *(He pokes gently at his side and winces in pain.)* Is this what a broken rib feels like? I think that big guy broke a couple of my ribs! And who was that girl? Did I hurt her?

WYSTERIA: That was Amanda Claypool. Normally, I'd say a punch to the face could only help her, but—

BIT GIRL: —But I think she broke her nose, Billy! She was bleeding all over the place and everyone else had run off; I had to come back to see if I could help her.

DR. FUNK: Ah, you're just making excuses! I'm talking about finding the Holy Grail and you're talking about—

DRAKE: —Aggravated assault! I mean, Dr. Marquette already wants to lock me up in a padded room and throw away the key. Can you imagine what she's going to want after this?

WYSTERIA: Drake, listen; it was an accident. Everyone ganged up on you and you were just trying to get away, that's all! Amanda's bad enough, but Billy Parker and his Nerd Herd are—

BIT GIRL: —Going to get arrested, probably. I heard Amanda talking to her dad and he was furious! All he could do was talk about calling lawyers and the cops and even the National Guard!

DR. FUNK: He can't get arrested! If he gets arrested, the feds'll just lock him up in one of their super-secret black sites and we'll never get any answers! Where are the others? Howling Tommy and Whiner?

BIT GIRL: Whiner took off. I think she's had enough for one night. Tommy's still out looking for the vampire kid.

DRAKE: They're all looking for me, Wysteria! I can feel it! The crowd, the cops; and who was that kid with the glasses and the crazy outfit?

WYSTERIA: I told you, that was Billy Parker. He thinks he's Buffy or somebody.

DRAKE: Buffy? As in *Buffy, the Vampire Slayer*? Oh, that's just perfect! Are you saying this guy wants to kill me?

DR. FUNK: You're killing me, Cheryl! You know that, right? This kid has died and come back to life! He has every answer I've been looking for my whole life and you want me to get upset about a broken nose and Whiner's hurt feelings?

BIT GIRL: Knock it off and calm down before I give you a nose to match Amanda's! This kid doesn't have any secrets! He hasn't been to the Other Side! He's just some poor screwed up kid who lost his mother — the same way you lost your sister — and he's just trying to figure it out. You should be helping him, not trying to make it worse!

DR. FUNK: Make it worse? Make it worse? There's only one thing in the world that'll make it worse —

DRAKE: I have to run away from home.

WYSTERIA: What?

DRAKE: Don't you see? If I stay, then you, my dad, you'll get held responsible for what I did! But if I run away, then I'm just a monster who went crazy and ruined everything.

WYSTERIA: *(Trying to remain calm:)* You're not a monster and you're not crazy. You're just confused —

DR. FUNK: Confused? About what? You're the one who's confused. You're the one who's trying to get me to surrender when the prize is almost within my grasp!

> *(Police sirens begin wailing in the distance and red and blue flashing lights begin strobing across the stage. To emphasize that they are not really standing together in the same part of the cemetery, Dr. Funk and Bit Girl should look off SR for the lights and Drake and Wysteria should look SL.)*

DR. FUNK AND DRAKE: What's that?

WYSTERIA: It's the police! They must have followed you here.

BIT GIRL: It's Five-Oh. That vampire kid must be closer than you thought.

DRAKE: You can't be seen with me! I've gotta get out of here! *(Running painfully off SL:)* Tell my dad I love him—

(He exits.)

WYSTERIA: Drake! Wait!

DR. FUNK: *(Checking his equipment:)* If the cops catch him, they'll stake him before I ever even get a chance to talk to him! We've got to catch him first, Bit Girl! Come on!

(He runs out and exits SR.)

(Bit Girl and Wysteria, both standing with their backs to one another on opposite sides of the stage, watching as their friends run off to do something truly stupid, turn to face the audience.)

WYSTERIA AND BIT GIRL: Well? What do I do now?

(Wysteria runs off SL and Bit Girl run off SR, both calling their friends' names. As they exit, the cemetery set moves off and is replaced by Drake's room.)

SCENE 3

(It is the next morning, about 3 A.M. Drake's room looks roughly the same as always, except the bed hasn't been slept in. As the lights come up, we hear Drake and Michael arguing offstage.)

MICHAEL: *(Off:)* You don't have to run, Drake. The sun won't be up for a couple of hours yet.

DRAKE: *(Off:)* I don't care!

(Drake bursts through the door to his room and throws himself onto the bed. For the first time, he is not wearing black. He is wearing an institutional-looking white T-shirt and gray sweat pants. His injuries have been bandaged, though his face is still puffy and bruised.)

I can feel it just over the horizon, trying to burn me! I have to get away!

(He covers himself with the bedding as Michael enters the room, slowly. He is exhausted.)

MICHAEL: Fine. Cover yourself up, hide under the bed. Brick yourself up inside your closet for all I care, but listen to me, will you? We have to talk about this.

(Drake doesn't say anything, simply lies there, facing the wall. Michael gets a chair and pulls it up next to the bed.)

Up to now, this whole thing has been pretty harmless to most folks. Oh they felt bad about your mom and felt bad that you were having such a hard time dealing with it, but you weren't actually trying to drink anyone's blood or peeking into anyone's windows, so everyone sort of felt like the only person you were hurting was yourself and it wasn't any of their business.

(He pauses to see if Drake wants to say anything.)

That's changed now. You attacked someone —

(*Drake turns over and glares at Michael.*)

DRAKE: I didn't attack anybody! If anything, she attacked me! She started it —

MICHAEL: But she's the one with the broken nose, son. And you're the one with her blood all over your shirt. She's telling everyone that you attacked her; that you were trying to drink her blood —

DRAKE: Attacked her? Those people attacked me! And I wasn't trying to drink anybody's blood. She can't prove that.

MICHAEL: She doesn't have to! She's got 30 people as witnesses and if they aren't outright agreeing with her story, they're not disagreeing with it either. Nobody is taking your side, son. Nobody except your friend Aimee —

DRAKE: (*Correcting him:*) Wysteria.

MICHAEL: Right. Wysteria. Whatever. And now you've been beaten up and arrested and spent most of the night in the hospital. And now we'll have to go to court and you'll have a record. And that girl's father is talking about suing us. The way the police are looking at it, you're an emotionally damaged kid who's spent time in a mental institution and thinks he's a vampire, for god's sake. That you had some sort of psychotic break and lashed out in a blind rage and tried to drink some poor girl's blood —!

DRAKE: I didn't try to drink anyone's blood! Please stop saying that. I'm sorry!

MICHAEL: (*Softly:*) I know you are. And I'm sorry too. I'm sorry that I've been so caught up in my own grief over your mom that I wasn't there for you like I should have been, that we weren't a family like we should have been. (*Beat.*) I miss your mom so much and I'd give anything to have her back here with both of us, but I've never blamed you for what happened and I will never blame you. I want your mom back, but I also want my son back and I promise I will move heaven and earth to find him.

(Vivian appears in the doorway as Drake stumbles up out of his bed to hug Michael. She is wearing a pair of jeans and a Philadelphia Eagles sweatshirt. Michael rises to meet Drake and they just hug for a moment.)

DRAKE: I love you, Dad.

MICHAEL: I love you too, son. No matter what.

VIVIAN: *(Entering room:)* Hello.

MICHAEL: *(Stepping away from Drake as he turns to her:)* Dr. Marquette. Any word?

VIVIAN: *(Stepping closer:)* Only what we already know. Since Drake has already spent several weeks this year in a mental health facility over his reaction to the loss of his mother, the Assistant District Attorney is afraid he may be a threat to the community and wants him examined by the police department psychiatrist to determine whether he was aware of his actions when he attacked the girl.

DRAKE: I'm telling you, I didn't attack anyone! I just swung my arm and she got in the way!

VIVIAN: Believe me Drake, I prefer your story. The only trouble is, you're the only one telling it. I'm afraid you might be in some real trouble here.

MICHAEL: So, what now?

VIVIAN: Now, you get a lawyer. Once the court opens in the morning, the ADA will get a court order remanding Drake to the Pennsylvania State Psychiatric Hospital for observation and an evaluation by their expert and they'll send both the police and an ambulance around to pick him up at ten o'clock in the morning.

DRAKE: Ten o'clock in the morning? I can't go out at ten o'clock in the morning! I'll burn!

MICHAEL: Isn't there anything you can do, Dr. Marquette?

VIVIAN: No. I explained the situation to the ADA, but he was unsympathetic. Once the court order is issued, it must be carried out. No exceptions.

DRAKE: But I'll die!

VIVIAN: Michael, could you excuse us for a moment?

MICHAEL: But wouldn't it be better if —

VIVIAN: No. Please wait outside. Perhaps you can find a blanket or something we can wrap Drake up in so he doesn't have to go out into the sunlight unprotected.

MICHAEL: OK, but I'm right outside if you need me, son. Right outside...

(Michael goes out the door and turns around to say something else. Vivian, following him, closes the door in his face. Again.)

VIVIAN: *(Turning back to Drake who has sat down on the bed with his head in his hands:)* That was very nice, what your father said about not blaming you. *(A beat.)* Why do I think you don't believe him?

DRAKE: I believe him. But...

(She takes the chair and places it near him.)

VIVIAN: *(Sitting:)* But?

DRAKE: *(Standing:)* But he doesn't know! He thinks I'm just a dumb, stupid kid! He doesn't know what I did!

(She stands and helps him to sit back down on the bed.)

VIVIAN: Sit down. You don't want to aggravate those bruised ribs any more than they already are. And what do you mean, "He doesn't know what I did"? Ever since I met you, you've been carrying this great weight, this horrible secret that threatens to eat you alive! What is it? What do you think you did that's so terrible?

DRAKE: Leave me alone!

VIVIAN: I can't leave you alone. Whatever it is you think you've done; whatever it is you're blaming yourself for, it's killing you! It is the single driving force behind your vampire fantasy and all your self-destructive tendencies!

DRAKE: Leave me alone! Please.

(She moves over to sit next to him on the bed.)

VIVIAN: Drake, I am trying to help you. I don't really believe you need to be committed, but that's what's going to happen unless you start participating in your own recovery.

DRAKE: *(Turning to face her:)* There is no cure for what's wrong with me. You might as well do the world a favor and just march me out into the sun and watch me burn!

VIVIAN: Getting upset doesn't help —

DRAKE: *(Crying:)* Of course, I'm upset, you moron! I killed my mother! I'm a monster!

VIVIAN: *(Speaking slowly and calmly:)* I don't believe that.

DRAKE: Then I'll make you believe it!

(He pushes her and begins walking toward her threateningly.)

You think I won't hurt you, break your nose like that stupid girl? You think I won't kill again?

VIVIAN: *(Backing away:)* If you'll tell me what happened, Drake, we can try to fix it.

(He pushes her again and continues advancing.)

DRAKE: Fix it? You make it sound like I'm a broken clock or something!

(Retreating, she puts the desk chair between them.)

VIVIAN: Drake, please tell me —

DRAKE: I'm not broken, I'm a monster! What do I have to do to prove that to you?

(He flips the chair out of the way. Backed up against the wall, she has nowhere to go.)

VIVIAN: Tell me what happened, Drake! Tell me!

DRAKE: *(Yelling and crying:)* I made my mother wreck the car! I hit her and she lost control and she died!

(He howls and grabs the desk chair, throwing it down away from Vivian and collapses onto the floor.)

Are you happy now? Do you understand?

(Michael knocks at the door, but doesn't open it.)

MICHAEL: *(Off:)* Drake? Dr. Marquette? I heard shouting, are you guys OK?

VIVIAN: *(Sitting on the floor next to Drake:)* We are fine, Michael. Everything is fine. Please go away. *(She waits until she is sure Michael is gone.)* Now, Drake, you must tell me the whole story. What happened on the day of the accident?

DRAKE: *(Standing slowly, not wanting to begin:)* Like I told you before, we were going into Philadelphia to get back-to-school clothes. Mom was talking about getting me some shirts and some jeans and I said I wanted these cool new basketball shoes. Mom asked me why, since I don't play basketball, and I said because they looked cool, and she asked me how much "cool" cost these days and I said a hundred and fifty dollars, and the fight started pretty much right there.

(Vivian gets up off the floor and sits on the edge of the bed.)

VIVIAN: And then what happened?

DRAKE: Oh, it got crazy pretty quick. She was yelling and I was yelling and she called me selfish and said I didn't understand how much money a hundred and fifty dollars really was, and I said something stupid, like "I'll bet it's worth a hundred and fifty dollars," and then I said if she really cared about me she'd get me the shoes and she said that if I really cared about her, I'd understand why she couldn't, and I —

(He stops, unable to finish.)

VIVIAN: What? What did you do?

DRAKE: I...I...

(He begins sobbing and puts his face in his hands. He says something, but we can't understand him.)

VIVIAN: *(Standing:)* You have to say it out loud, if you want to truly be free of it. What did you do?

(He looks up at her helplessly, his face covered in tears.)

DRAKE: I called her a bitch. *(He shoulders slump, as if finally saying this out loud is crushing him.)* I didn't mean it! I was just so mad! And then she swatted me on the leg — it didn't even hurt — and without thinking, I just reached out and shoved her and then, bam, we hit that other car and went in the ditch, and...

VIVIAN: *(Crossing to him, but not touching him:)* Drake, the man who hit you that day was drunk. Blind drunk, to tell the truth. His wife had left him the night before and took their baby with her and he had been drinking all night and all that day. His blood alcohol level was almost triple the legal limit! By the time he hit you, he had already side-swiped two other cars and torn through somebody's garden. He told the police that he was *trying* to hit somebody; that he was hoping he'd die.

DRAKE: But he didn't die, did he? Instead, my mom and I did. Because of me. It's all my fault.

(*She puts a hand on his shoulder, finally daring to touch him.*)

VIVIAN: No. The accident still would have happened even if you and your mother had been singing show tunes that day. It's not your fault.

(*He shakes off her hand and steps away SL.*)

DRAKE: But it is. We died and it was my fault and now I'm paying the price. I'm finally the monster on the outside that I always was on the inside and when the police come, I'll walk out into the sunshine and burst into flame and finally get what's coming to me.

VIVIAN: I can't imagine you believe that.

DRAKE: No? I want to believe it! I should have died that day instead of her! It shoulda been me in that ditch and she should still be alive with my dad! I just want my mom back!

(*Suddenly, he collapses into her arms and she holds him.*)

I just want my mom back...

(*The lights dim and go out.*)

SCENE 4

(As the lights go down, the curtain closes on the bedroom, and the front stoop of the house from the beginning of the play is placed center stage in front of it. The crowd from the movie theatre stands both SR and SL of the stoop and three or four dressed as police and ambulance attendants stand SR of the stoop. As the lights come up, Penelope enters SL with Amanda in a wheelchair. In addition to her broken nose, which is seriously taped and bandaged, Amanda's arm is in a sling and her leg is bandaged from foot to thigh. She also has a bandage wrapped around her head and band-aids stuck to strategic locations on her face and arms. Also, her eyes are both blackened from the broken nose and she still has dried blood on her lip. In Amanda's lap is a big stack of Celebration of Positivity and Goodwill fliers. As Penelope and Amanda enter, they continue an argument that began offstage.)

PENELOPE: *(Crossing toward Center with Amanda:)* Seriously, ma'am, this isn't right. I don't know how you're possibly going to get away with this!

AMANDA: Get away with what? I was attacked!

PENELOPE: You weren't attacked and you know it. You may have been accidentally hit in the nose, but the rest of this—

AMANDA: *(Shooting a dangerous look at Penelope:)* "The rest of this" I got at the hospital, when *somebody* decided to park me at the top of the stairs and not set the brake on the wheelchair!

PENELOPE: I said I was sorry!

AMANDA: Sorry? You broke my leg, you moron!

PENELOPE: *(Sarcastically:)* Well then, I guess I'm really sorry! *(Under her breath:)* Too bad you didn't break your jaw...

AMANDA: What?!

PENELOPE: Nothing! Just saying how sorry I am. Again.

AMANDA: If this doesn't work, I'll definitely give you something to be sorry about! All of this— *(Indicating the wheelchair and bandages:)* —is just set-dressing for the TV crews. While we were at the hospital and you were taking your dear sweet time finding a machine that sells my favorite brand of lemon water, I had to drag myself out of my sick bed to call my daddy's secretary to make her call all of the protest groups his ad agency uses to add drama to their publicity stunts to get a crowd down here so that the newspapers and TV stations will come and I can get on TV for my 15 minutes of fame and buy my way into the college of my choice!

PENELOPE: Ma'am did you ever stop to think that it would be a lot easier to get into college if you'd just studied in high school, like the rest of us?

(Penelope pushes Amanda DSR as they continue arguing in pantomime.)

(The Geeks enter from SR from behind Amanda and Penelope. Upon seeing the police, Dr. Funk holds the collar of his jacket up so that they can't see his face.)

BIT GIRL: You see, Billy? I told you there'd be a crowd. And cops! This is a really stupid idea.

DR. FUNK: *(Taking her by the shoulders, he is wound-up and somewhat frantic:)* And I am tired of explaining to you, Bit Girl, how important this is! I will not let them sweep this kid up in their black helicopters and never see him again! Not when I'm this close!

WHINER: *(Looking around excitedly:)* There's helicopters? Where?

DR. FUNK: Shut up, Whiner. *(To Bit Girl:)* The answer to the greatest paranormal secret of all time is right behind that door and I will not let them sweep it under the rug and try to convince us all that there was a gas leak and we were seeing Pink Elephants or something!

WHINER: *(Tugging at Dr. Funk's sleeve:)* There can't be any elephants, Billy. Where would they put them?

TOMMY: Shut up, Whiner. *(To Dr. Funk:)* But what are we going to do, Boss? Those are cops over there. Real ones. With real guns. All we have are water pistols filled with holy water, and I'm not sure the guy who blessed them was really a priest.

DR. FUNK: We'll have to make a diversion, Tommy. When the kid comes out, Bit Girl and Whiner will pretend to get into a fight or something and while the cops are breaking them up, you and I will swoop down like avenging eagles and snatch the kid away!

WHINER: Now we've got eagles? How about "lions and tigers and bears, oh my!?"

TOMMY, DR. FUNK AND BIT GIRL: Shut up, Whiner!

WHINER: Fine! Nobody ever tells me nothin'!

(Bit Girl sees Amanda and Penelope DSR, still arguing with one another. She crosses to them and the rest of the Geeks follow.)

BIT GIRL: *(Seeing Amanda and taking a couple of steps toward her:)* My god, Amanda, what happened to you?

AMANDA: That idiot vampire kid attacked me, is what happened! He tried to suck my blood and broke my nose!

TOMMY: You're in a wheelchair for a broken nose?

(At this point, Wysteria enters SL from behind the crowd and excuses her way to the front.)

WYSTERIA: *(Looking toward the house:)* Excuse me, have they brought Drake out yet?

AMANDA: *(Making Penelope turn the wheelchair to face Wysteria:)* I know you! You were with the vampire kid. You're his—

DR. FUNK: *(Interrupting:)* His what? His Renfield? His minion? His evil little henchman?

AMANDA: *(Looking at Dr. Funk like he's crazy:)* Well, I was going to say "his girlfriend," but whatever.

WHINER: *(To Bit Girl:)* Ooh, I told you they were dating!

BIT GIRL: *(Almost kindly:)* Shut up, Whiner.

AMANDA: *(To Wysteria:)* This is all your fault!

WYSTERIA: My fault? How is any of this my fault?

(They start to argue, but are interrupted as the door to the house opens and Drake, Michael and Vivian come out. Drake has a large blanket over his head and is hunched over, trying to stay out of the sun. He is still bandaged from before. As they reach the bottom step, the policemen and ambulance attendants move in to escort them and they begin crossing SR as the crowd moves in and begins to take pictures and yell out questions. Wysteria tries to go to Drake, but once again, she is blocked by Tommy.)

DR. FUNK: Bit Girl, Whiner, we need that distraction. Start fighting. Now!

WHINER: *(Crossing her arms and pouting:)* I'm not doing nothing. You guys are mean to me.

DR. FUNK: Never mind! I'll do it myself.

(He runs around Tommy and wraps one arm around Wysteria's neck and shoulders from behind. Wysteria cries out in surprise.)

I've got the girl!

WYSTERIA: Drake!

DR. FUNK: I said, I've got the girl! You have to do what I say!

BIT GIRL: Billy, no!

DRAKE: No! You leave her alone!

(Without thinking, Drake rushes Dr. Funk, losing his blanket. He pulls Wysteria free from Dr. Funk's grip and grabs him by the shirt front.)

If you ever touch her like that again, I swear—

WYSTERIA: Drake! You're out in the sunlight!

DR. FUNK: *(Surprised:)* You're out in the sunlight...

(Drake looks at himself and up at the sun and faces Wysteria.)

DRAKE: I guess I am. *(To Wysteria:)* I just—I saw him grab you and I—I just didn't want to be the reason anybody else got hurt.

(Wysteria hugs Drake and he hugs her back. Vivian and Michael cross to Drake and Wysteria.)

WYSTERIA: Well, thanks for saving me. It was very brave.

DRAKE: *(Surprised:)* It was? Oh, yeah, I guess it was. Brave, I mean. *(Straightening up, trying to appear manly and confident:)* That's just how I roll.

WYSTERIA: *(Laughing:)* My hero.

(She hugs him tightly and after his initial surprise, he hugs her back.)

AMANDA: *(Pointing to Drake:)* Wait a minute! What do you mean, he was brave? I'm the victim, here! I'm the brave one!

PENELOPE: Shh, ma'am. You shouldn't try to talk in your condition.

AMANDA: Why can't I talk? There's nothing wrong with my mouth.

PENELOPE: *(Holding up a fist behind Amanda's head:)* Not yet there's not, ma'am.

DR. FUNK: *(To Tommy:)* Where were you? I could have used some help in there.

TOMMY: Sorry boss, my mom always told me that we don't hurt girls. They smell too pretty.

(Dr. Funk looks away, embarrassed, as Vivian speaks to Drake.)

VIVIAN: Well, Drake. You've had a big day.

DRAKE: Yeah Doc, I guess I have. Would you call this a breakthrough?

VIVIAN: *(Smiling:)* We'll see. I'm still going to have to take you to the hospital, though. We can't violate the court order.

DRAKE: That's OK. I think I can use the rest.

MICHAEL: *(Giving Drake a hug:)* I'm really proud of you, son.

DRAKE: Thanks, Dad.

WYSTERIA: Drake, can I ride with you to the hospital?

DRAKE: Sure. That'd be great.

(Drake, Wysteria and Michael talk in pantomime as Vivian sees Dr. Funk.)

DR. FUNK: *(Embarrassed:)* Hi, Dr. Marquette.

VIVIAN: *(Crossing to him:)* Hello, Billy. I wasn't sure you were going to speak to me.

DR. FUNK: Yeah. Sorry I've missed my last...30 or 40 sessions.

VIVIAN: My door is always open. I still have your appointment time available. Shall I see you on Tuesday?

DR. FUNK: *(Shrugs.)* I dunno. Maybe.

VIVIAN: I'll look forward to it.

(Michael and Wysteria take a step SR as if to exit.)

DRAKE: I'll be there in a minute, Dad. *(Crossing to Vivian and Dr. Funk:)* We haven't officially met yet. *(Putting his hand out to shake:)* I'm Drake.

DR. FUNK: I'm Doctor— *(He grins sheepishly and shakes Drake's hand.)* I'm Billy. Billy Parker.

(Vivian pats Drake's shoulder approvingly and joins Michael and Wysteria.)

DRAKE: I heard about your sister. I'm sorry.

DR. FUNK: Yeah. Sorry about your mom.

DRAKE: What did you want with me, anyway?

DR. FUNK: You know something? I'm not really sure. Answers, maybe? I don't know.

DRAKE: I know that feeling. Look, I'll tell you what. I'm absolutely sure I don't know anything more about anything than you do, but when I get back, I'll talk to you for as long as you want.

DR. FUNK: Sounds good, man. Thanks.

(Drake smiles and joins Michael, Wysteria and Vivian. They exit together SR, with the police and ambulance attendants following.)

All right, Geeks, let's reconnoiter back to the Geek Cave—

BIT GIRL: *(Interrupting him:)* You mean your parents' basement?

DR. FUNK: *(The sheepish grin again:)* Yeah. Let's go to my house and re-think our mission statement.

(He begins crossing SL to exit with Tommy and Bit Girl. Whiner doesn't move. Dr. Funk notices Whiner isn't coming and stops to call to her:)

Hey, Whiner? Um, Dawn? You coming?

WHINER: *(Still hurt:)* Maybe. In a minute.

(Satisfied, the Geeks continue exiting SL.)

DR. FUNK: This time, I'm thinking we search for the Abominable Snowman!

TOMMY: I'm thinking we search for lunch. I'm starved!

(They laugh and exit and the crowd begins dispersing to exit SL and SR as well, until only Whiner, Penelope and Amanda are still on stage. Penelope is trying to help Amanda get settled in the wheelchair.)

AMANDA: *(Noticing that everyone is leaving:)* Hey, wait! Where are you all going? You can't leave! This is all supposed to be about me!

PENELOPE: *(Trying to calm her:)* Ma'am, you're getting too upset...

AMANDA: *(Pushing her away:)* Oh, just go away and leave me alone, Penelope! As always, you're just butting in, making things worse! This is supposed to be about me! My daddy and his lawyer said that if I get a crowd over here, and get myself on TV, all banged up and pitiful, everyone would feel sorry for me and realize what a hero I was for capturing the crazy vampire kid and maybe I'd get a medal. I'd get my scholarship! *(Pitching a real fit:)* Come back here, people! This is my day and you're ruining it! You're supposed to feel sorry for me! I'm supposed to be famous!

PENELOPE: *(Sadly:)* Oh, we feel sorry for you alright...

(Penelope crosses center to be met by Whiner.)

AMANDA: Penelope! Where are you going? You can't leave; get back here!

WHINER: Hey. How come you hang out with her?

PENELOPE: I don't know. How come you hang out with him?

WHINER: Good question. I'm Dawn.

PENELOPE: Penelope.

(They shake.)

You want to go get some ice cream?

WHINER: Sure.

(They exit SL as two police enter SR and approach Amanda. Amanda doesn't see the police yet.)

AMANDA: Penelope? Where do you think you're going? Come back here this instant!

POLICEMAN #1: Excuse me, miss? Are you Amanda Claypool?

(Amanda whips her head around, startled and immediately regrets it.)

AMANDA: Ow! What are you doing, sneaking up on an invalid like that? Are you trying to put me back in the hospital?

POLICMAN #2: We're sorry to bother you, miss, but could you answer the question? Are you Amanda Claypool?

AMANDA: Of course, I'm Amanda Claypool, you idiot! Who else would I— *(Something occurs to her.)* Oh, are you here to help me? Did my daddy send you to take me to get my picture taken for the paper? Am I going to be on CNN?

POLICEMAN #1: Uh, we don't know anything about that, miss. We're here about the angry mob that was gathered here a few minutes ago.

AMANDA: Wasn't that great? I got them here all by myself! Of course, they were supposed to stay —

POLICMAN #2: Miss, are you admitting that this demonstration was all your doing?

AMANDA: Of course! Who else could have done all this? Frankly, after the whole Celebration of Positivity and Goodwill thing, this was a piece of cake!

POLICEMAN #1: Wait a minute, miss. Are you also taking responsibility for the Celebration of Positivity and Goodwill?

AMANDA: Isn't it just the best? Between that bogus hippie love fest and being attacked by a fake vampire, I'm gonna get my ticket to Yale, for sure! Or Princeton. I haven't really decided yet.

(The two policemen look at each other knowingly and Policeman #1 takes out a pair of handcuffs as Policeman #2 takes hold of the wheelchair.)

POLICMAN #2: *(As Policeman #1 tries to cuff her:)* I'm afraid you'll have to come with us, miss.

AMANDA: *(Fighting off the cuffs:)* What? What are you doing? You can't arrest me; I haven't done anything! I'm a hero! Why are you doing this to me?

POLICEMAN #1: I'm sorry, miss, but you're under arrest for two counts of unlawful assembly, one count of inciting to riot, two counts of holding a meeting without a permit, filing a false police report, obstruction of justice...

AMANDA: *(Kicking and hitting them.)* You can't do this! Do you know who my father is? I am Amanda Isabella Claypool and I am a hero!

POLICEMAN #1: ...resisting arrest, assaulting a police officer...

(Amanda howls, throwing down her big stack of fliers.)

Littering...

(Amanda continues to complain under dialogue.)

POLICMAN #2: You have the right to remain silent. Please. Anything you say can and will be used against you in a court of law —

AMANDA: I want my daddy!

(Lights fade and... CURTAIN.)

(At the end of curtain call, Dr. Funk leads the cast in the following rap:)

DR. FUNK: WELL, YOU CAME TO THE SHOW AND YOU SAW OUR —

ALL: PLAY!

DR. FUNK: YOU WEREN'T SURE YOU'D LIKE IT, BUT YOU STUCK AROUND —

ALL: ANYWAY!

DR. FUNK: WE THANK OUR MOMS AND OUR DADS AND OUR TEACHERS —

ALL: TOO!

DR. FUNK: NO NEED TO HANG AROUND, 'CAUSE THIS SUCKER IS —

ALL: THROUGH! *(Chanting as they exit:)* THROUGH, THROUGH, THIS SUCKER IS THROUGH! NO NEED TO HANG AROUND 'CAUSE THERE'S NOTHING TO DO!

(Lights out. End of play.)

The Author Speaks

What inspired you to write this play?
I was doing set design and dressing for a theatre group I'm a member of, for a production of *Radio TBS* by Mark Landon Smith and in the show there's a one-line, throw-away joke about the local community theatre doing a play called *Dracula of Transylvania*. The joke is that the local print-shop misread the title and misprinted the poster to read, *Dracula of Pennsylvania*, instead. It was a so-so joke that got a so-so laugh, but I couldn't get that misprinted title out of my mind. What would a "Dracula of Pennsylvania" be like? Would he be Amish? Would he really be a vampire? My drama students at school were after me to write something for them that really had some meat to it and spoke to where they were and how they felt and what they were afraid of and they immediately responded to the story once they heard my idea. Once I figured out Drake's central tragedy, everything else just grew naturally out of that.

Was the structure or other elements of the play influenced by any other work?
No, but there's a scene at the beginning of Act II, where two different pairs of actors are having two different conversations that interweave and connect with one another in both dramatic and comedic ways that I remember from an old comedy routine when I was a kid. Once I got the idea to use it in *Dracula of Pennsylvania*, it really got Act II off to a good start and allowed me to look at the story so far from two different perspectives at once.

Have you dealt with the same theme in other works that you have written?
Not to this degree, perhaps, but it's difficult to write for

teenagers and not write about their struggles with loneliness and belonging and guilt and trying to find out how they fit into the world. My other work, *Techies, Band-a-thon!* and others deal generally with teenage characters moving forward to find their places in the future, but in *Dracula of Pennsylvania*, Drake and Billy and Wysteria and all are trying to find ways to not only move forward into the future and what life has in store for them, but also to find a way to fit comfortably in the framework of their own families and their own skin. The human condition is never so raw and emotion is never held as close to the surface as it is when we're young.

What writers have had the most profound effect on your style?
I am extremely influenced by David Mamet and Aaron Sorkin, who both have such an amazing command of the English language that they can create the most beautiful sentences, filled with such thoughts and emotions and spirit; the words climbing and cascading over themselves in the most perfectly crafted way and then beat you over the head with them as if they were a bat and your head was a mailbox. I am also in awe of Neil Simon's comic timing, Neil LaBute's audacity and the way Tracy Letts can exaggerate and pull what we consider "normalcy" all out of whack and then hold it up in front of our noses to show us that it still looks just like us after all.

What do you hope to achieve with this work?
Dracula of Pennsylvania doesn't really talk about suicide, but it's a topic that is certainly written large in the subtext. I would hope that this play would encourage people to be more open about the things they are going through and the challenges they are facing and to understand that you never have to face things alone as long as you're willing to let someone in. Also I'm trying to shine a light on how guilt can be a good thing; it

can keep us honest and humble, but how it can also be a poison that can eat us alive and destroy everything we hope for. I would hope this play would begin a conversation among people that will enable us to recognize the truly frightening number of people out there who are truly miserable and who feel totally and completely alone.

What were the biggest challenges involved in the writing of this play?
There was a great deal of research that had to be done about mental illness and how the law treats minors when they get in trouble. I also had to speak with a couple of therapists about how they do their jobs and interact with their patients. From a story-telling standpoint, it was important to me that, despite the humorous way they dress or present themselves, Drake, Wysteria and the Agents of GEEK be identifiable as real people with depth and history. I spent a great deal of time writing personal bios and little character vignettes so that when the time came to actually write the story, I could put down each character, not just in a way that's honest and true to their journey, but with the same flow and texture as real life.

What are the most common mistakes that occur in productions of your work?
They don't get my name big enough on the marquee. Seriously, the one thing I have noticed most in productions of my work is a lack of attention to proper pacing. Not that I'm writing farces here, but there is certainly a rhythm to the way I write and a speed at which I intend the dialogue and action to move forward. I'm the first to admit that much of my work is dialogue-heavy and if you can't find that pacing, things can get bogged down really quickly and that's not good for the play, the production, the actors or the audience.

What inspired you to become a playwright?
I've always liked telling stories but really hate writing narrative. I enjoy the back and forth of dialogue and tend to rush through the narrative to get to what I considered to be the good parts. As such, playwriting is perfect for me. I started writing skits for an after-dinner theatre group I started in college and my theatre professor, Judith Lewis, urged me to try writing something a little bit bigger and more in keeping with what I was learning as an actor. I wrote my first play, *Behind the Clowns*, shortly thereafter and the rest, as they say, is a frightening cautionary tale about the dangers of not staying focused and the crippling effects of procrastination.

How did you research the subject?
Well, of course, I Googled a lot. Seriously, I don't know how we lived before the internet. Otherwise, I spoke with a couple of real-life therapists about their methodology and techniques, as well as what was and wasn't acceptable therapeutic behavior. I also took advantage of my old grad school roommate who is now a Juvenile Court judge about how the legal system treats minors and the kinds of sentences they could receive. Mainly though, I spent a lot of time talking to my drama students about their own feelings of alienation and how they would react to a character like Drake and how they would react to the world if they were Drake. It was quite eye-opening.

Shakespeare gave advice to the players in *Hamlet*; if you could give advice to your cast what would it be?
Have fun. For a subject as somber as the one in *Dracula of Pennsylvania*, there are some truly fun and memorable characters. Don't just concentrate on the "drama" of it all; go nuts with the comedy portions as well. In my production the

kids playing the Agents of GEEK really went all out creating their weapons and other ghostbusting doo-dads, and my Angry Mob really bonded over their sign-making parties. Like Mary Poppins' "Spoon Full of Sugar," the most dark and dreary subjects find a much more receptive audience when you place them in the light.

About the Author

A 35-year stage veteran, **Don Goodrum** was born in Tennessee and raised in Mississippi, where he got his first taste of the spotlight as The King of the Calendar in his second grade play. Don moved onto the church play circuit and managed to turn a Best Actor win in a One-Act Play Festival into a theatre scholarship to Mississippi College. At MC, Don began writing in earnest and saw several of his plays produced. After college, Don wound up married and on the radio, a career choice that kept sharpening his comedic and writing skills for the next 32 years. Don retired from radio in 2006 and began writing once again and has seen productions of many of his plays, including *The Devil and Daniel Webster,* an adaptation of the classic story by Stephen Vincent Benet. He lives in Florida.

About YouthPLAYS

YouthPLAYS (www.youthplays.com) is a publisher of award-winning professional dramatists and talented new discoveries, each with an original theatrical voice, and all dedicated to expanding the vocabulary of theatre for young actors and audiences. On our website you'll find one-act and full-length plays and musicals for teen and pre-teen (and even college) actors, as well as duets and monologues for competition. Many of our authors' works have been widely produced at high schools and middle schools, youth theatres and other TYA companies, both amateur and professional, as well as at elementary schools, camps, churches and other institutions serving young audiences and/or actors worldwide. Most are intended for performance by young people, while some are intended for adult actors performing for young audiences.

YouthPLAYS was co-founded by professional playwrights Jonathan Dorf and Ed Shockley. It began merely as an additional outlet to market their own works, which included a substantial body of award-winning published and unpublished plays and musicals. Those interested in their published plays were directed to the respective publishers' websites, and unpublished plays were made available in electronic form. But when they saw the desperate need for material for young actors and audiences—coupled with their experience that numerous quality plays for young people weren't finding a home—they made the decision to represent the work of other playwrights as well. Dozens and dozens of authors are now members of the YouthPLAYS family, with scripts available both electronically and in traditional acting editions. We continue to grow as we look for exciting and challenging plays and musicals for young actors and audiences.

About ProduceaPlay.com

Let's put up a play! Great idea! But producing a play takes time, energy and knowledge. While finding the necessary time and energy is up to you, ProduceaPlay.com is a website designed to assist you with that third element: knowledge.

Created by YouthPLAYS' co-founders, Jonathan Dorf and Ed Shockley, ProduceaPlay.com serves as a resource for producers at all levels as it addresses the many facets of production. As Dorf and Shockley speak from their years of experience (as playwrights, producers, directors and more), they are joined by a group of award-winning theatre professionals and experienced teachers from the world of academic theatre, all making their expertise available for free in the hope of helping this and future generations of producers, whether it's at the school or university level, or in community or professional theatres.

The site is organized into a series of major topics, each of which has its own page that delves into the subject in detail, offering suggestions and links for further information. For example, Publicity covers everything from Publicizing Auditions to How to Use Social Media to Posters to whether it's worth hiring a publicist. Casting details Where to Find the Actors, How to Evaluate a Resume, Callbacks and even Dealing with Problem Actors. You'll find guidance on your Production Timeline, The Theater Space, Picking a Play, Budget, Contracts, Rehearsing the Play, The Program, House Management, Backstage, and many other important subjects.

The site is constantly under construction, so visit often for the latest insights on play producing, and let it help make your play production dreams a reality.

More from YouthPLAYS

Techies by Don Goodrum
Comedy. 25-35 minutes. 5-6 males, 3-4 females (8-9 performers possible).

Overachieving high school senior Tony Sullivan just wants to get through one more production so that he can move on to Harvard and the rest of his life. But with overdramatic actors, overmedicated teachers and overprotective parents seemingly aligning to thwart his every move, will the show go on? Will Tony? A comic look at one of life's most important transitions and a loving tribute to the unsung heroes of the stage, the kids who sit in the dark and make the magic happen.

The Superhero Ultraferno by Don Zolidis
Comedy. 100-110 minutes. 6-50 females, 6-50 males (12-90+ performers).

Now that nerds have taken over the world, it's imperative that all popular kids learn everything they can about comic book superheroes. Join two nerds and a crack team of actors as they race hilariously through the world of tights-wearing crimefighters, from the 1960s TV Batman to the soap opera insanity of the Fantastic Four to a bizarre, German opera of Spiderman. Also available as a one-act.

Warriors by Hayley Lawson-Smith
Drama. 40-50 minutes. 4 females, 1 male.

Not every hero gets a song or the cheers of the crowd—or even acknowledgement. In Zordana's land, a hero fights bravely in the open field, destroying monsters and dark magic. In Amy's world, her hero is the sister who takes care of her. For Maddie, her hero is her brother, who may tease her mercilessly but loves her dearly. As tragedy threatens to consume their separate worlds, only in coming together can they battle back the dark.

Dear Chuck by Jonathan Dorf
Dramedy. 30-40 minutes. 8-30+ performers (gender flexible).

Teenagers are caught in the middle—they're not quite adults, but they're definitely no longer children. Through scenes and monologues, we meet an eclectic group of teens trying to communicate with that wannabe special someone, coping with a classmate's suicide, battling controlling parents, swimming for that island of calm in the stormy sea of technology—and many others. What they all have in common is the search for their "Chuck," that elusive moment of knowing who you are. Also available in a full-length version.

The Exceptional Childhood Center by Dylan Schifrin
Comedy. 25-35 minutes. 2-4 females, 2-3 males (5-6 performers possible).

Reggie Watson has been accepted into the right preschool. He's set for life…as long as he can make it through the one-day trial period. But when desperation breeds disaster and his future hangs in the balance, Reggie and his band of quirky classmates may just discover things about themselves that school could never teach them.

Dancing With Myself by Leanne Griffin
Dramedy. 35-45 minutes. 7 females.

Goth Girl. Moody Chick. Gamer. Cheerleader. New Kid. Jock. Nerd. Seven high school girls and the labels they've been forced to wear. But in this innovative, award-winning dramedy, whether it's sports or a sleepover or the classroom or a school dance or the ups and downs of daily life, they'll use music as their inspiration to break free of the stereotypes and discover the unique identity they each possess.